Test

"I have found Rhonda's writings to be educational while remaining light-at-heart. Rhonda has a wonderful way of addressing day-to-day situations, which to some may seem 'common sense,' but in reality are not normally put into practice. Recalling some of the tips she has put before us has helped me to make wiser decisions before taking action—not only within the office but at home and in other situations as well."

Bernardine Ketelaars, MDiv
Executive Assistant to Bishop Ronald P. Fabbro, C.S.B.
Diocese of London

"Common sense is just not that common any more. With all this new technology sometimes things (like common sense) get deleted. The little reminders Rhonda puts in this book are great to share with co-workers, family, and friends.

It might just make this big scary world just a little bit nicer." ☺

Sue Fera
ECE Leader
Northern College

"Common sense is seriously lacking in the workplace today, but Rhonda uses it in all of her articles. That's why it is so easy to put her ideas to use both at work and in everyday life."

Patty Buckner
Executive Assistant/Manager Administration
Ontera

"Your writings are so influential. By putting your experiences in account when you write, you let me know that you are a common-sense person. I am happy to say that I enjoy being a client and look forward to turning common sense into common practice and achieve superior performance."

Sheila Clifford
EHS Administrative Assistant
3M Company

"Rhonda is always filled chock full of good, sensible advice that is relevant not only in the workplace but in day-to-day life as well. The humorous stories and anecdotes she uses make this one publication I look forward to receiving and sharing with friends and colleagues."

Lynne Spackman, CPS/CAP
York Region

"Thanks for the stress relief you provide with your short, clear, concise newsletters. Since discovering and subscribing to your monthly e-mails, I have thoroughly enjoyed taking 'sanity breaks' to refresh and be reminded of the common sense ideas and practices which make our daily lives easier and better, both at home and in the office."

Joan L. Leeson
Administrative Coordinator
Children's Oncology Group

"I always enjoy the up-to-date and relevant articles Rhonda shares. As someone with almost three decades of admin experience, I am finally looking forward to retirement in a few weeks. Many of your articles have encouraged me—some have confirmed that what I was doing was correct—and others just made me happy to be an admin professional."

Joyce Rourke
Administrative Assistant
Peel Region

"Not only here in the corporate world are new policies being written just about every other day, but you see it daily in the news by way of a new law or ruling. Recently we heard that no more texting while driving will be allowed…does that really need to be made into law? To me that's just good common sense. Our new policies and laws are always in response to something incorrect, inappropriate, or just plain idiotic that someone else did. It doesn't seem fair that everyone should be subjected to insulting and indiscriminate laws and policies because of one person that made a mistake or a bad decision. Thankfully, most of us can still rely on common sense!"

Dawn Ward
Coventry Health Care

"I like your common sense information because you use simple and concise language and the content is quite educational, current, and applicable. You definitely provided interesting information to your readers."

Ada Lee
Region of Durham

"I always look forward to Rhonda's advice. It is always common-sense themed and they definitely help keep us on the right track. Can't wait for the next one."

Susan Brimer, CPS/CAP
Boys & Girls Club
Town of Missouri

"Rhonda brings up topics we have all thought of or complained about and tells us in her straightforward yet humorous manner how to deal with the every day annoying issues of life. Her common-sense advice, when put into practice, makes us better employees, bosses, co-workers, friends, and partners."

Sharon Desserud
Ministry of Child & Youth Services

Common Sense is *NOT* Common Practice

How to Ensure You are **ON THE RIGHT TRACK**
to Better Business Sense and Success

Rhonda Scharf

Roberts & Ross Publishing
COLORADO • FLORIDA • USA

Common Sense Is NOT Common Practice

How to Ensure You are **ON THE RIGHT TRACK**
to Better Business Sense and Success

by Rhonda Scharf

ISBN: 978-0-9822015-3-4 (paperback)
First Edition

Printed in the United States

PUBLISHER	Roberts & Ross Publishing
	ENGLEWOOD, CO
	(303) 762-1469
	SANTA ROSA BEACH, FL
	(850) 622-5772
	RobertsRossPublishing.com
BOOK DESIGNER & PRODUCER	**COVERS & INTERIOR**
	Sheila J. Hentges
ILLUSTRATOR	**COVERS & INTERIOR**
	Shauna Grant

Dedication

This book is for all my readers.

I hope you enjoy reading it
as much as I enjoyed writing it.

Acknowledgements

How can I possibly share my common sense with you and not acknowledge where it came from. To all of those who influenced me as I was a child, and as I continue as an adult, thank you. Thank you to all the teachers who had an impact on me in school—teachers make a difference. Thank you to anyone who was ever in a position to give me advice (even if I didn't take it). I learned (sometimes the hard way).

To Warren Munn, the man who hears my common sense daily (even when he doesn't want to), thank you for listening, thank you for agreeing to see my point of view (even when you don't want to), and thank you for your unconditional support.

Special thanks go to my mother, Audrey May, and her parents, Stanley and Jessie May, for teaching me to make common sense my practice. To Gordon and Sharon Scharf along with Elisha and Hazel Scharf, where would I be without you and the common sense you have instilled? My in-laws, Leland and Iona Munn, have had an impact in my life with their common sense in a very short period of time as well that will travel with me for the rest of my time. Parents and Grandparents have always played a major role in my life, and I pray that will continue for a very long time.

As a parent I hope that I can continue to share my common sense in a helpful way to my children, Christopher and Patrick Finniss along with Victoria and Leland Munn. I hope that I can influence you with the same positive energy that my parents influenced me with.

For each of you who have taken the time to ask questions during my speeches and training programs, via email or telephone, I thank you as well. The lessons we have all experienced is where the knowledge comes from.

Thank you one and all for the lessons I have learned.

Table of Contents

Introduction   1

PART ONE   **5**   *Office Etiquette*
                    6   Every Day Can be *Thanks-Giving* Day
                    9   Do You Put in a Full Day at Work?
                   12   The Importance of a Professional Workplace
                   15   What *NOT* to Wear to Work
                   20   Rules for Working in a Cube Farm
                   24   Don't Answer That!
                   27   Ever Been "Nervous?"
                   30   False Sense of Security
                   33   What Are You Attracting?

PART TWO   **39**   *Communication Basics*
                          for Office Harmony
                   40   Good Customer Communication
                           is Good Customer Communication:
                           It all Starts with Service
                   44   Red Light and Green Light Words
                   50   If You Want My Advice—Too Bad!
                   53   Do You Interrupt Others?
                   57   You Can Stop Awfulizing (and prevent
                           others from doing it to you)
                   61   How do You Handle Compliments?
                   63   Do You Sound Credible?
                   71   Voice Mail. Tips to Guarantee
                           a Positive Impression
                   75   Frustrated? Don't Call Me!
                   79   Are You Listening?

PART THREE   83   *How to Make Nice in the Sandbox:*
The Importance of
Teamwork in the Workplace

   84   The Sense of a Goose

   86   The Common Commitment

   88   Taking Initiative

   92   Begin with the End in Mind

   96   We Can Learn a lot from *The Apprentice*
       Or, Whom Do You Trust?

  101   Procrastination…Don't Create Dis-ease
       with this Disease!

  105   Solution or Band-Aid?

PART FOUR   111   *Life and Work.*
A Juggling Act or a Balancing Ballet?

  112   Do You Bring Your Work Home with You—
       or Your Family to Work?

  115   Work Less, Live More

  118   Are You Prone to STRESS?

  120   A Facelift for the Mind:
       Reduce Negative Stress

  125   Let's Get Busy Doing Nothing!

  128   Are You Sleeping Enough?

  131   Do You Know How to Relax?

  133   The Benefit to Relaxation:
       It Recharges Your Batteries

  136   The Pursuit of Balance

PART FIVE   **143** *Success is Celebrating You*

144 How Do You Define Success?

148 Are You Good Enough?

150 Are You Ignoring Your Own Thirst?

153 Stuck in a Rut?
     Here's How to Get off the Nail

159 Get Your Mojo Back

162 You are Either Living or You are Dying.
     Which are You Doing?

165 You're Never Too Old

167 Do You Celebrate You?

Introduction

Why is one person successful and the other is not? What is the difference between a gold medal and a silver medal at the Olympics? Why do some people seem to just enjoy life more than others?

I get asked those questions all the time and even get paid to share the answers. What I often find is that the answers are simple; you already know them. They aren't rocket science or take a degree in quantum physics to get them. No, the best answers to these questions come in the form of plain old, every-day common sense. The common sense your grandmother tried to instill in you. The common sense that we see missing everyday at work, on the bus, on the television and in the newspaper (and sometimes in the mirror).

If you want to be successful, if you want to be happy, and you don't want to go through life "settling" for anything other than the gold medal—all you need to do is practice what you already know!

The answer is right in front of you, but first you must get your bad habits out of the way. You are the difference between gold and silver, between happy and trapped, between mediocre and successful. It is you who is sabotaging you. It hurts to admit it, but fortunately it is easy to fix.

As you share my journey on common sense, be completely honest with yourself and ask "Do I do that?" Be truthful. Learn from the mistake. It is okay to make mistakes in life, just don't lose the lesson.

The stories that you're going to read about in here are taken from my experiences with people who continue to lose the lesson. Unfortunately, because they follow common practice and not common sense, they will never be successful, never be happy, and they are never going to "get it!" I want you to be one of those in the "successful" camp. I want you to "get it," and you will—*if you are honest, if you are willing, and if you practice a little common sense.*

PART ONE

Office Etiquette

We go to school to study and learn. We go to college to become qualified in what it is we will do with our entire lives. Our identity is in huge part determined by what you do, who you do it with, and how you do it. The truth is, we spend most of our waking lives at work. We also all know that to be true, but why is it that people continue to plod through life not realizing the impact they have on others? They could be so much more successful and happy with a little awareness, a little compassion and understanding, and a whole lot of common sense!

Unfortunately, we live in a visual, material world, and no matter how smart you sound, if you don't present yourself in a professional way, you're not going to be perceived as professional. While we all know that common sense, it seems, gets thrown out the window these days when it comes to how we handle ourselves around our office mates—from the way we dress to the state of our desk. I want you to wake up and look in the mirror—and what follows is just some of my random thoughts along these lines…

Every Day Can be Thanks-Giving Day

What has happened to our culture that we don't say "thank-you" anymore?

I was in a drug store recently and made a sizeable purchase. At the end of the purchase, I said, "thank-you." I really think that the cashier should have said "thank-you," as I'm sure—considering how much I spent—that I contributed to the profitability of the store that week. Instead, I was the one who said "thank-you," but instead of the cashier saying "you're welcome," her response was—you guessed it—"uh-huh."

At the bank this morning, I held the door opened for the gentleman behind me. He didn't acknowledge my courtesy.

However, the bank was late in opening this morning, so when I had to get a money order, the bank teller waived the fee because I had to wait for them. She said to me "this is a thank-you for your patience this morning." That was nice—customer service as it should be. Sadly, this is the exception not the rule.

Please and *thank-you* were the two of most important words I learned to use when I started working as a teenager. It has contributed to my success so far. Thanks, Mom and Dad, for teaching me manners.

Thanking the person who served your coffee is polite, as is thanking the person who made the coffee in your office, even if they made it so they could have a cup. Say "thank-you" to the person who holds the elevator, delivers your mail, and picks up your garbage. Say "thank-you" to your spouse for just coming home tonight, and thanks to your kids as they come home safe and sound as well. Say "thank-you" to the person you look at in the mirror, because some days that's the only thank-you we get.

When you are saying "thank-you," make sure the words reach your eyes and make eye contact with the person you are thanking. Be sincere because that means as much, or more, than the words you use.

Say "thank-you" to your support team at work. They should thank you as well, as hopefully you are a joy to work with. In fact, what the heck. Go crazy and say "thank-you" to everyone at work whether they support you or not and truly mean the words you are sharing. And on Mother's Day, we know we need to thank Mom for everything she has done for us over the years. Same is true for Father's Day.

Why do we need to be reminded to say "thank-you" one day each year? Shouldn't we go through life with a thankful mentality? Let's start right now and put ourselves on-the-right-track by saying "thank-you" several times each day. Say "thank-you" to co-workers, family members and complete strangers.

Try it and you'll be amazed at how much better you feel, how much more positive life is, and how your smile stays on your face. Don't focus on those who say "uh-huh" or don't acknowledge your thank-you, and return the thanks to yourself by saying "Thank-you, (insert your name) for being the more polite and respectful person today."

Count how many times you say "thank-you" today, and of course, be sure to add the equally correct "you're welcome" when someone says "thank-you" to you.

Most of all, I thank you for taking the time to read this book. Thank you if you pass it on to someone who normally wouldn't purchase a book like this, and thank you for allowing me the privilege of writing, speaking, and sharing my life with you.

Do You Put in a Full Day at Work?

My teenaged son, Christopher, works at a golf course. His shift starts at 4:00 p.m. If I am driving him to work, he is in a complete state of panic if he's not at the golf course by 3:50. He is worried that he will be fired.

In the past, I had an office temp help me with a seminar. Her scheduled starting time was 8:00 a.m. She arrived at 7:52 and apologized for being early, and then excused herself "to relax" until eight.

Why is it that my teenager gets it, and yet this full-grown adult does not?

To me, common sense says starting time means "start no later than." It does not mean the time you walk through the door, or the time you pull into the parking lot. Starting time implies that you have already filled your cup of coffee, already checked your horoscope online, read the newspaper and said hello to your friends. It means you are "starting to work."

Unless it is understood that you work on a flex-time schedule, it is not a flexible start time; it is not 8 a.m.*ish*. You are being paid to work thirty-seven hours a week (or whatever your agreement is) and you are expected to be at the office for certain times.

The same goes for breaks and lunch. You get fifteen minutes. Not seventeen. Not twenty-five because you worked through lunch, but fifteen.

There was a time when everyone had to punch a time clock to indicate they were in the office and working at their starting time. The clock kept track of breaks, lunch, and when you left. If you punched in late, your paycheck was adjusted.

Although most of us don't have to punch in to a time clock today, we should act as though we do. Let's assume you arrive to work at 8 a.m. By the time you hang up your coat, get your coffee and boot up the computer it is probably 8:15. At lunch, you like to go to the gym, and your gym class is forty-five minutes long. It takes a few minutes to get changed, a few minutes to freshen up, and perhaps your lunch break becomes sixty-five minutes long. Your bus picks you up outside your office at 5 p.m. sharp. If you miss that bus, you have to wait forty-five minutes for the next one, so you start cleaning up your desk to leave around 4:40, and sneak out around 4:52 each day.

This adds up to about thirty minutes a day that you are cheating your company. Thirty minutes a day at fifty weeks a year equals twenty-five hours a year, or almost a full week of work. How much money do you make in a week? Would you be willing to pay someone an extra week per year for work they didn't do?

Most people assuage their guilt with rationalizations: "I work through breaks," "I work overtime" or "I take work home." Fine, but that is what you are doing freely of your own volition. You were hired to work eight to five. You decided to offer these extra bonuses to your firm, but who gave you the right to remove time from your regular schedule? Unless you agreed with your supervisor that you have flexibility, do not assume that you have this flexibility. I guarantee your co-workers notice it, are annoyed by it, and complain about it. People remember the negative (she shows up ten minutes late every day). They will not assume you are working ten minutes extra every day to compensate, especially if they are not.

Sit down and have a chat with your boss and arrange some flexibility if it is necessary. That way, everyone agrees to your work hours and you will have nothing to feel guilty about.

I'm thrilled that Christopher insists on being at work early. It means I've done something right. He has the appropriate work ethic and attitude and realizes that having a job is a gift, not a right. I am sorely disappointed in adults who don't "get it" and nickel and dime their company on working hours. Common sense teaches you to offer more than what you are asked to do, not the other way around. You earn a paycheck for the hours you work and the work you do. No one owes you for what you didn't deliver, for displaying a poor work ethic, and for not having the right attitude. They certainly aren't people I would hire again.

The Importance of a Professional Workspace

Close your eyes and walk into your office or cubicle. When you open your eyes, look at your desk as if it doesn't belong to you. Now describe the person who owns this desk. Do they seem professional and competent, or frazzled and disorganized? Now remember that this is your desk, and think about what message it's sending about you.

I am a pretty good housekeeper. My mom was obsessive-compulsive about keeping a neat house. She vacuumed daily, she ironed everything, and everything was put away when we were finished with it. She drilled into me how important it is to be neat and tidy. Now, I keep a fairly clean house, and although I do not vacuum every day, I still iron everything. I want to give the impression to friends and family that although I am a full-time worker and mom, I've "got it together." Not always true, but always the message I want to send.

I was recently visiting relatives who were not brought up under my mother's rules. The dishes were piled in the sink, the laundry was on the floor, and the table was covered with clutter. Without me even realizing it, I recoiled, wondering what on earth could make someone keep house like that. I even commented on it to my husband, Warren. How could they know that we were coming and not bother to clean up?

Ha!

I was thinking about this later, as I was walking into my office. The couch was filled with briefcases, boxes, books, and clutter.

The desk was invisible under a pile of papers. There were Post-It notes and scraps of paper with writing on them everywhere.

If I were hired to work with someone who had an office that looked like mine, I would assume they needed lessons in time management, organization, and most certainly, professionalism.

I am organized, I do manage my time fairly well, and I like to assume I am professional. However, my office certainly didn't look that way. And using the same yardstick I'd used with my relative recently, judging by my office I would have said that I was disorganized, unprofessional and not good at my job. As I pointed out above, people do judge by appearances. Once you accept that fact you can move forward and deal with it.

QUICK TIPS TO GETTING ORGANIZED

I recognize that not all of us grew up with obsessively clean mothers, and not all of us are naturally tidy. So here are a few tips on getting your work space in order.

- Use color-coded folders, Post-It notes, pens and anything else that will help you see at a glance where to find what you need when you need it.

- Pile if you must, but try to avoid collecting piles of information. Perhaps invest in a vertical hanging file folder (which by the way I had... sitting empty on my desk).

- Put things away. Even if you have messy drawers, put your pens, staples, extra notes, paper clips and other bits away. It won't take long to get them out of an (hopefully organized) drawer.

- Clean up before you leave each night. Many people keep different hours than you, and by leaving your desk in a messy state, you are leaving a message about yourself, even when you are not there.

- If you're really at a loss because your desk is piled so high, start with just one pile of papers, or one heap of clutter. Figure out how you're going to deal with it, do so, and once you've put it all away, you will find that the other mess isn't so hard to deal with.

I understand busy. I understand clutter. I even fall victim to it. However, busy and cluttered doesn't have to mean unprofessional and unorganized. You want to give the message at work that you've got it together.

Make sure your desk is reflective of your personality and reflective of your professionalism and efficiency. It shouldn't be reflective of your work load. Just because you have a lot to do doesn't mean it should look like a tornado hit your desk.

Make sure your desk matches the message you are intending to send.

Busy = Good. Cluttered = Bad.

Check the success of your assessment with a couple of honest co-workers.

Common sense would tell you to keep your desk and workspace professional looking. Use your common sense and keep your best interests in mind, and keep your desk looking neat and tidy.

What **NOT** to Wear to Work

Since we're on the topic of "how things look," let's take a minute and examine how we dress.

Have you ever watched the TV show *What Not to Wear* on TLC? I do—and I am often mortified by what others think is acceptable to wear to work. We are all paid professionals. Shouldn't we look like it?

I think there should be a course given to every new employee on what exactly it means to come to work dressed professionally. I know that I'm not alone in this thought. I'm not sure when it started, this idea that we can wear to work what we wear at home. I remember looking at a picture of the women who worked in the airplane factories during WWII. Even though they were working on planes with heavy tools in their hands, their hair and makeup were perfect and their clothes were surprisingly clean and neat given what they were doing. Now they may have been gussied up because they were getting their picture taken, but I've seen too many similar pictures, so I think they really did look like that. I'm not saying that we need to have our hair set and our lipstick perfect even when we're doing a dirty job at work. What I am saying is, common sense tells us that we should make an effort to look nice.

I also understand that it is a very touchy subject in many workplaces, but here's my list of "don'ts," no matter how formal or casual your office is.

THE SHAGGY DOG LOOK

When you go to work with your hair wet, you are sending out a very apathetic message. Would you ever go on a date or to an interview with your hair wet? So why would you go to work with wet hair? Get up fifteen minutes earlier, or wash your hair the night before, but don't show up at the office with wet hair.

PONYTAILS

To compound that mistake, some people put their hair in a ponytail (especially if it is wet) and then go to work. A ponytail is what I do to my hair when I don't want to fix it, or when I'm going to the beach; it's not a professional look. If you take the time to make it look nice, use a nice hair accessory, and generally put effort into it, then it can look professional. But if your attitude is "I'll just stick my hair in an elastic because I'm running late," what are you saying about yourself? Nothing good, that's for sure.

CROCS ARE FOR SWAMPS

Crocs are a particular favorite of many people. I do not own a pair, nor will I. I am told by those who wear them they are incredibly comfortable. I like comfortable, but not at the cost of the look of the footwear. They look terrible! Slippers are comfortable and I don't wear them to the office either! Facebook has a group you can join called, "I don't care how comfortable Crocs are, you still look like a dumba—." No matter how much you love them, Crocs are not professional footwear for the office, period. Not ever. Some hospitals have even banned them because they are not safe or hygienic. I don't even want to think about what some of them must smell like! If you've been wearing Crocs (with or without socks), put them in the closet during working hours, and know that you have comfy footwear to put on when you get home.

RAIDING THE HAMPER

T-shirts with slogans don't belong in the workplace. Jeans with rips or holes in them don't belong in the office (and really, are jeans professional wear?). Clothes with stains on them, clothes that are faded, clothes that should be pressed but aren't because you didn't have time, shouldn't appear in the office. Clothes that smell need to be washed, not worn to work.

TOO MUCH INFORMATION

Shirts with spaghetti straps don't belong in the office; they belong on the dance floor. Also, I never want to see your bra straps. If I can see your bra straps, go get another shirt. And this goes double for thong underwear—I don't want to know that you wear a thong. That is just too much information. I don't want to be able to see through your shirt and see your bra either. I understand that there is quite a selection of bra styles and colors out there, but you shouldn't be putting that on display at work. If you are wearing a white shirt, a black bra is just wrong.

I could go on and on about what not to do at work. But it's also rude to bore people, so here's a checklist that both men and women can follow when it comes to dress etiquette:

- If you would wear it to go to a dance club or a party, you shouldn't be wearing it to the office.

- If, when you bought it, it was pressed and clean, that is how the garment is meant to be worn (as opposed to dirty and wrinkled).

- Lingerie is for a different profession; in the office, I don't want to see it.

- Wet hair and "beach hair" are inappropriate in the office.

- Shoes that are for work do not include running shoes (unless you run in the office), plastic shoes, those dollar-store plastic flip flops or party shoes (rhinestones or really, really high heels). Please keep your footwear in good condition, fix the lifts and soles and polish them occasionally.

- Put some effort and thought into what you wear to work. Just because it is "the only thing that you have that is clean" is not enough thought.

- You should never have to make excuses for what you are wearing. If you need to go somewhere else after work, bring a change of clothes.

- The more cleavage you choose to show, the lower your credibility will sink.

- Sexy is not a look you should be going for at work.

- While a shirt and tie are not always necessary, shirts with collars are appropriate in virtually every office.

- Your shirt should always have sleeves.

- Appropriate jewelry usually means limiting the amount you wear. More is not always better.

- Have a look at your nails. If you have chipped and chewed-away polish, please take it off. Either polish needs to be perfect or it shouldn't be there at all.

While it is not realistic to go to work dressed "interview appropriate" every day for most people, have a look at your outfit before you leave home. Would you feel comfortable if you were pulled into a last-minute meeting with the senior executive team? Would you be dressed appropriately to meet an unexpected client?

Make sure you aren't the next person being followed around the office with a hidden camera so that others can sit back and laugh at your choices! Choose with common sense, look in the mirror and see if Mom would approve, and you'll be fine.

Rules for Working in a Cube Farm

We do some of the silliest things while at work. We get comfortable with our co-workers, and we start considering our workspace an extension of our home. When that happens, we often cross that invisible line between professional and personal. When we work in close proximity with others it is almost as if they become like family. You love family and you love to hate family. Families share too much information, they speak their mind too freely but they love unconditionally so all is forgiven.

Your co-workers (especially if you work in cubicles) are too close, and you end up sharing too much information, end up speaking your mind too freely. But unlike your family, all is not forgiven, because ultimately they are not family.

Have you crossed the line?

You work in a limited area with a lot of other people. You come to know a lot about them, and they about you. The little things they do drive you insane, and you can be sure the reverse is also true.

When you work in a cubicle, there are certain rules that you need to follow and certain levels of awareness you need to have so that everyone can peacefully co-exist in that confined space.

PRIVACY

You have none. Just because you can't see other people while in your cube does not mean that you are alone. You are not. Every phone conversation you have will be overheard by many people—especially the three others who share that square with you. Gossip is rampant in every office, and you don't want to be the topic of conversation because you had a private conversation in a very public place.

I remember this happening to me about twenty years ago when I worked in Toronto. I spent eight hours a day in my cubicle, loving the team I worked with, and since I am highly social, I thought a cubical concept office was a great thing. That is, until the day I had a very private (or so I thought) conversation with my mother about where I'd been the night before. The timing was bad, but Mom was worried about me, so she called me at the office. For a few moments, I forgot I was at work and I got into my private and personal conversation, unaware that several of my colleagues were silently following along. Since they could only hear my side of the conversation, that left quite a bit to their imagination, and they were all too happy to fill in the gaps themselves.

I was mortified when I was questioned later by a coworker. I was embarrassed that my conversation had been actively listened to, and that further conversation and speculation about my personal behavior was occupying the thoughts and actions of my coworkers.

But I learned my lesson. Now I save those personal conversations for home or private locations. Every time a friend, child or parent calls us at work, someone in our office makes mental notes in the invisible file they keep on us. The bottom line is that it's impossible to have a private conversation in a cubicle.

VOLUME

Your cubicle is designed to absorb sound. If you have papers stuck to the wall, they will deflect sound, making your conversations even louder to other ears. Remove anything that is on the wall that did not come with the original design so at least your conversations aren't as loud as they might be otherwise.

When talking on the phone, speak down into your desk instead of spinning around in your chair (making yourself comfortable) and looking into the office space or out the window. Speaking out of the cubicle will make your sound travel and even more people will hear your conversation. Even if you are talking about work and the information is not private, it is not respectful of other people for your voice to be so loud. Speaking into your cubicle will absorb sound.

Since cubicle areas usually contain many people, the white noise throughout the office will creep up through the day. This will cause you to speak even louder so you can hear yourself think. If you get accused of speaking in a loud voice outside your office (by family and friends) this could be the culprit. Be very aware of your volume.

Listening to an iPod or earphones or even a radio (which is terribly disrespectful as that sound travels even at a low volume) throughout the day also skews your volume levels. Teenagers are a perfect example. As soon as they take off their iPod they are yelling. Are you doing the same because you are drowning out the white noise in the office by listening to music? Constant noise (or music) in close proximity affects your awareness of your volume level. We talk louder to be heard over the sound, and it is often too loud.

NEATNESS

You don't have much space, so organization really counts. The smaller the space you have the faster you will make an impression. Is your impression the one you want to convey? Are you neat enough for your small space?

MAGNETS

Do you have stuff at your desk that entices coworkers to visit? Do you keep candy or the funny comic strip that brings people by to visit you? If you do, while it may be great for your social life, it is impairing the working space for those around you. Don't invite people to visit you to chat at your cubicle, and if it is work-related, keep it short.

HAPPY BIRTHDAY

Cubicles are terrible for customer service. When someone is on the phone with a client and the cubicle next door is singing "Happy Birthday," it sends a very bad customer-service message. The same is true for boisterous laughter and other loud conversations. For some reason our customers don't want to think that we have too much fun at work.

Working in a tight space with so many others requires us to really think about how our working habits affect others. Most of our bad behavior is done innocently enough, but creates tension in the workplace that does not need to be there.

Pay attention, lower your voice and call your mom from home.

Don't Answer That!

Well, since we're on the subject of what not to do at work, I had to throw this in.

I was in the airport recently (along with thirty-five of my new best friends) waiting for a maintenance delay to be over so we could all get to where we wanted to go.

One gentleman in particular was not happy to hear that yet another delay had been posted for our flight. He expressed his frustration to the gate agent. You know and I know (and I'm willing to bet that even he knows) that the gate agent can't do much about it, but he was trying to get some answers.

In the middle of him explaining that he had to show up at his military base no later than midnight to sign in, the agent's personal cell phone rang. Ignoring the man and his frustration, she dug her phone out of her purse, and answered it. She said nothing prior to answering the phone to the extremely frustrated gentle-man at the counter. He was left completely speechless by her rudeness.

The other day I was going to a business meeting in an office tower, signing in with the concierge, and the same thing happened to me. His cell phone rang and off he went to have a personal chat while I waited for him to finish.

And while I was having lunch last week with a seminar participant, her cell phone rang, and she answered it, proceeding to carry on a conversation with her mother.

What has happened to the world that a ringing cell phone stops all business from happening? How on earth did we conduct our personal lives during working hours prior to having cell phones?

Work hours are for work. We don't need to be in constant communication with our friends and families while we are at work, and it shouldn't interrupt our working day. I'm sure if the CEO of your company was standing in front of you, you wouldn't answer your cell phone (at least I hope you wouldn't). Your customer is no less important than the CEO because after all, she's the one who affects your company's bottom line.

Emergencies are different. If it's an emergency, it is certainly acceptable to use the company phone and call your family member. Everyone will agree to that.

However, why do you need to have your cell phone on your desk for you to receive personal calls while working? You don't.

Give your family your office phone number in case of an emergency, and keep your cell phone turned off while you're at the office. If your kids need to let you know they are home safely, they can call the office line or send you an e-mail. If your mom wants to chat, speak to her when office hours are over. And you shouldn't be calling the radio station during working hours to enter a contest, regardless of what phone you use.

At the airport, the gate agent should have left her phone ringing in her purse. In any case, she shouldn't even have had it on, since I can't imagine a scenario in which it would ever be appropriate for her to have a personal call where all the passengers could listen in.

She should have saved her personal calls for her break time, when she was out of the view of customers and co-workers.

The concierge at the office tower should have not answered his phone either. There was plenty of time once the foyer was empty for him to continue his conversation if his workload allowed it (but I'm pretty sure he had other things to do).

My lunch mate had every right to answer her phone—it was lunchtime. However, it was incredibly rude for her to continue her personal conversation, with me sitting there trying not to listen.

Put yourself in your companion's shoes. Would you appreciate someone ignoring you while they carried on a personal conversation in front of you? I'm sure you wouldn't.

Etiquette is all about manners, and good manners are all about paying attention to how your actions affect others. In an office situation, your etiquette meter should always be turned up to "high." What you say and how you say it. What you wear, and how you carry yourself, all matter in an office environment. So pay attention, use good judgment, and you will be appreciated, even admired, in your workplace.

Ever Been "Nervous"?

Sometimes "etiquette" seems to fly out the door, however, through no fault of our own. We want to act as professionally as we look and follow proper etiquette, but sometimes that's hard to do. There is one example of when etiquette takes a back seat but with good reason. It has to do with getting nervous. When you're nervous, you often make mistakes and that can seem unprofessional.

Seriously, do you ever get really nervous about doing something? So nervous that the butterflies are not only flying in formation, they are also doing something like synchronized swimming in your stomach? Why is it that sometimes we can do a task that doesn't make us even skip a beat, and other times it immobilizes us from doing anything at all?

You can use many examples when we talk about nervousness: in a job interview, delivering a speech at work, even reading bible verses at church. You know the feeling that starts in the pit of your stomach, makes your hands all clammy and yucky, throws even normal breathing patterns right out the window...and sleep isn't an option the night before.

I teach a great course on Presentation Skills. It is primarily for people who have to make presentations as part of their job. I was teaching it in Edmonton and we were discussing the nervousness that goes with giving a presentation. Someone in the class asked me why they got so nervous—especially in front of a group of peers. Although this is a very normal question, my answer was slightly different this time.

I think that we are nervous because we care. We care about not making fools of ourselves; we care about making sure that our content makes sense; we care about doing a good job; we care about the job we are applying for; we care about the company, the people and the accuracy of the information. If we didn't care, we wouldn't feel nervous, would we?

Have you ever noticed that if you have to present in front of people you know, it is much harder than speaking to people you don't know? Even for me, a professional speaker, this is the case. When someone I know is in the audience there is much more on the line.

I'm currently in a huge state of nervousness about a presentation I'm about to make. Why? Because it matters. Does it matter any more than the countless other presentations I've made before? Probably not. What does matter is the fact that my audience is filled with my peers. I care about doing a good job. Now I know, and you know, that we regularly do a good job, right? So why does this matter so much? More importantly, what can we do about it?

Well, acknowledge what you are nervous about. Is it about looking stupid? If that is the case, be sure that you know your material the best you possibly can. If you do that, you won't look stupid. If you have to give a presentation at work, be prepared, practice the night before, and if you stumble a bit, so what? Just keep your cool and move on. When I read in church, I make sure that I am very comfortable with the words in the passage because I don't want to pronounce any of them the wrong way.

What else are we nervous about? Sometimes we are nervous about being judged by our peers. Fair enough, right? And we may be, and there is nothing we can do to change that. So, if we know we are being judged, shouldn't we make sure that there is nothing they can legitimately criticize?

We are also nervous about the crazy things in life. Things like having toilet paper sticking out of the back of our pants; like saying something completely inappropriate; like your voice mysteriously disappearing just before it is your time to speak. I worry about those crazy things, too, but I always do a "check" before it is my turn in the spotlight. These kinds of things have happened to others before, and not a single person has died as a result of it. Eventually, it makes for a very funny story.

Nervous energy is a legitimate thing. It is there. Ignoring it does not make it go away. We must deal with it rationally. Figure out what we are nervous about and ensure that you have done everything you can to avoid that situation. When the event is over and you look back on it, always ask yourself "Would I have done anything differently if I had the situation to live all over again?" If the answer is no, great! There isn't much to be nervous about and practice will make it perfect. If the answer is yes, then implement your suggestions and try again!

Good luck! Remember that nervousness is a good sign. The more you feel it, the more you care about doing a good job and that is never a negative sign.

False Sense of Security

Hmmm, to be honest, I don't know if what I'm about to tell you is office etiquette per se, but in our technological world, it is vital for you to work efficiently and well. What I want to talk about here has to do with backing up your data.

Remember when computers were introduced into the workplace? We were told we would have a paperless society. But on average today, nineteen copies of each original document are made. Hardly a paperless society! I think all that paper gives many of us a false sense of security. We assume there are multiple copies of everything floating around, and that nothing can really get lost.

Bad assumption.

I lost data, important data. However, my false sense of security allowed me not to panic.

Then I let the panic set in.

My laptop died. I should have seen it coming. I had just bought the latest version of Microsoft Office, and I had set aside Thursday to do a complete system backup, prior to installing it. On Monday morning I started to notice that the system was slowing down. By noon it had died.

Even then I didn't panic. I knew there were multiple copies of my documents floating around in lots of places. My assistant, at the time, had a desktop computer in the office that she worked on. She must have had some stuff on that system, right? What I didn't think about was all my e-mail that I had stored in folders so it was handy for me as I traveled. I had completely forgotten about my priceless files containing my clients' addresses (although the database is backed up regularly on my home office system). All my e-mail to-dos had disappeared. And to cap it all off, my digital photos were gone. Most were not work-related, but clearly these were extremely valuable!

In my storage room, I had copies of all the workbooks I have created for clients. So I was not totally lost, but it meant that I had to recreate those workbooks, which was no small task.

I was smart enough to have my large database of clients on a separate computer (on which backups were regularly done), and I had an old backup of files on the main office computer, which would save some time. But I realized that I was far too comfortable, knowing that I had paper copies; I neglected to do regular backups of that system. I really hadn't given any thought to the time that might be involved recreating large volumes of documents.

This is not the first time a computer has died on me, and it won't be the last. In spite of that, I've been far too complacent about making backups and paid a heavy price for that.

Are you doing the same at your office? Are you relying on the automatic backups that are done at your company? How often do they do them—do you even know? What happens if the server crashes? What about your own personal hard drive or confidential documents; do you regularly back those up? And when is the last time you backed up the files on your home computer? Just in case you need a reference file to walk you through the process: www.microsoft.com/athome/moredone/backupfiles.mspx will help you.

And even though this is a book primarily about work, I have to mention this: last year my uncle lost his house and its entire contents to fire. Providing the insurance company with the necessary details about everything that was in the house was an incredible amount of work. Have you ever done an inventory on your home?

What about your wallet? Do you have copies of your credit card numbers, your driver's license, health insurance number and social insurance number? What about a copy of your passport? It is far too easy to lose a purse or wallet, and far too difficult to remember what we carry around. I know you have paper copies of your bills, but can you lay your hands on those copies quickly, so you can easily contact those companies?

Call it stress management, proactive style. It would be a huge amount of work to recreate all this information, and it's so much easier to do it now. I paid the price for assuming my copies were easily accessible, and for not taking into account the time and stress involved.

On a personal note, take some time to do backups of your photos, important documents, insurance papers and credit card numbers. If you can, store them in a safe-deposit box at your bank. At work, make sure you back up *all* your files regularly. Heaven forbid some-thing negative should happen to your files or papers; but if it does, at least reduce some of the stress it would create by being prepared.

What Are You Attracting?

Well, I've given you some common sense advice on what to wear, how to handle yourself, even what to do with your files—all with the intent of helping you succeed better at your job by doing the things you know you are supposed to do (but if you are like most, you haven't been doing them). Now I'm going to switch gears a little in this final piece of part one. I thought it would be a good idea to take a good look at who you're hanging around with at work. Depending on who you're with, it can make or break your day, and if you are happy at work it makes everything better! Here's some simple, yet very telling questions, you can answer for yourself: Do you like the people you hang around with at work? Do you even *like* the people you *work* with? We spend so much time with them, we didn't get to pick them, and they have an amazing impact on our lives—whether you want them to or not.

You might be thinking that you don't have a whole lot of control over the people you're sharing an office with. But consider this, just because you "office" with them, doesn't mean that you have to hang around with them during lunch and on breaks.

There has been a lot of talk over the last few years about the "laws of the universe." Recently there has been a lot of focus in books and talk shows about these laws. Some of these laws are: The Law of Clarity of Mission, The Law of Give-and-Take, The Law of Expectation and The Law of Attraction.

A couple of weeks ago I was being coached on my marketing materials. We discussed many of the different laws, but the one that stuck with me the most was the "Law of Attraction," which states that "like attracts like."

My coach, Deanna, applied that to marketing. While she was doing that, I was thinking about how it also applies to workplace relationships. What can we learn from the Law of Attraction?

If like attracts like, then I am surrounded by people who are like me. You've heard the expression, "If you want to fly like an eagle, stay away from turkeys." Essentially, it means that we tend to hang around people who are like us. To get some insight into ourselves, we can look at who we are attracting—those people we like to spend time with and those who like to spend time with us.

If we find ourselves constantly surrounded by people who are negative, perhaps we are exuding a bit more negativity than we realize. One of the ways to keep negativity away is to constantly turn it around and make it positive. The negative person does not want to hear the positive. She is comfortable with the negative; it is what she gives and what she wants back. Many of us believe that the negative person is dealt with effectively if we just listen and don't give her any feedback. What we often don't realize is that no feed-back is just the same as enabling feedback.

If your child said to you, "tomorrow I am not going to school," and you ignored the comment, your child might assume he had your implicit permission not to go to school.

If your negative person gives you negativity and you choose to say nothing, you may be implying that you agree, or at the very least, are not disagreeing with what she says. If like attracts like, then we may be attracting negativity by not being positive.

Another way the Law of Attraction works in our lives is in how much we like our jobs. If we love what we do and consider it a privilege to get paid to do what we do, then we typically will spend time at work with people who also like their job. We tend not to spend time with people who hate what they are doing because it is very draining to us emotionally.

If you are spending time with people who hate their job, you will re-evaluate what you love, listen (almost in spite of yourself) to what your co-workers are saying, and may even feel that some of their comments are justified. Just by being surrounded by constant job dissatisfaction you will automatically start to question your own job satisfaction.

LIKE ATTRACTS LIKE

It seems that some people get all the breaks in life. They are in the right place at the right time. They get to meet all the right people. They get all the promotions and they seem to get all the glory. Is it that these people are just lucky? Or could they be attracting what they exude?

Deanna made me look at my marketing materials to see what message they were sending and what types of clients I was attracting. Perhaps you also need to have a look at what, and who, you attract. Are you attracting people just like you? Are you happy with it? If not, change what you are sending and you will change what you receive.

If you think about it, the way we present ourselves has a lot to do with how we're perceived. I know I touched on hard subjects to confront, but remember, just because it's common practice does not mean it's common sense. One of my mom's favorite sayings to me when I was a teenager was, "If all your friends jumped off a cliff, would you jump off one too?"

No, of course I wouldn't. Make sure you are not jumping off the proverbial cliff at work either.

PART TWO

Communication Basics for Office Harmony

We're probably sick to death of hearing that we need to have good communication skills no matter what we do for a living. There's something interesting in that complaint—communication is important, it is the basis for understanding, and good communication can dissolve almost any problem. So why is everyone tired of hearing about it? Perhaps it's because it's the age-old problem. Everyone jumps on the "what's wrong" bandwagon; few offer real, viable solutions.

What follows is not any "big picture" stuff. Rather it looks at the little, even random miscommunications that happen everyday that drive us all nuts! I want to point them out to you so that when you find yourself in a compromising communication situation, you'll have some tools ready to smooth over whatever tsunami is threatening the peace of your day.

Good Customer Communication is Good Customer Communication: It All Starts with Service

Why is it that some people are unaware of the impact their actions cause to others? Why do other people always come up with an excuse or blame for their actions, when they really can control the outcome? Why do people not take responsibility? What do these questions have to do with communication? Everything.

A couple of years ago, I experienced one of the worst customer-service examples I could possibly imagine. The Christmas vacation that had been booked for eight people had just been cancelled, a mere three days prior to our scheduled departure. There were now four very upset children, four very angry adults, one very confused dog, and a completely invisible vacation management company—invisible because it refused to communicate.

The vacation management company did a lot of talking at us. They told us that the house we had booked to rent had been sold. They chose to ignore the fact that we signed a contract with them and not the owner. They chose to ignore the fact that they are responsible for ensuring good customer service; they chose to blame the owner. They did not want to engage in good communication with us because they absolutely did not want to take responsibility for what happened. They just kept blaming everyone else.

When we work in an office, we are not an island unto ourselves. We have a responsibility to help each other, work together as a team (a concept I tackle in the next section) so that the customer—the end user—is happy. When the customer is happy, you generally have a better chance of keeping your job, *and* to be able to do all that effectively, we have to be able to communicate to each other. Sounds like common sense doesn't it?

First point I want to make about all of this: common practice is, sadly, all about blaming others. When something goes wrong in the office, it's someone else's fault—too many people are too quick to take that road. Instead, think about taking the high road. Own up to what you've done and work to find a solution to what has happened.

Second point: If you think this doesn't apply to you, think again. Why is it that some people are unaware of the impact their actions cause to others? Why do other people always come up with an excuse or blame for their actions when they really can control the outcome? Why do people not take responsibility?

One of the quotes I use in my Customer Service program is "All Roads Lead to the Customer." It amazes me how few people in an organization are aware of this fact. What I find is that the people who deal directly with the customer are aware they are in a customer-service role. Anyone who does not speak to the customer directly feels that he or she has no impact on the customer. This is not the case. Everyone in an organization has an impact on the customer, whether it is direct or indirect.

The person who processes the bills has a direct impact on the customer. The customer could be depending on that check to pay the mortgage. Should they decide not to process the payment, it could be an example of very poor customer service to the person expecting the check.

The person who answers the telephone and directs the phone calls has a major impact on customer service. If he or she makes a habit of cutting off callers or being rude, you can be sure the customer feels it, and that it will affect the business.

I once heard a story I love, and which I love to tell. When a reporter asked a man who worked for NASA what he did there, he responded: "I helped put the first man on the moon." The man being interviewed was a janitor. Did he help put a man on the moon? Yes; by ensuring that the others could do their jobs. His actions had an indirect impact on the astronauts who landed on the moon.

Third point: Good communication makes for good working relation-ships. Tom Peters in his book *In Search of Excellence* said, "96 percent of the labor force is involved in service positions, either internally or externally."[1] And really, 96 percent seems low now because the point here is, you are in a service position whether you recognize it or not. If we're in a service position, then that means we all have customers in some form or another.

Now when that was released, 96 percent was considered a very high and even controversial statistic. That was before what I call "The Customer Service Revolution." Back then (over twenty-five years ago, can you believe it?) the only people who had customers were in retail or a restaurant environment—certainly not government or monopolies!

Now as we fast forward to today, the 96 percent seems to be a very low percentage. Doesn't everyone have customers? And if we all have customers, shouldn't we all maintain those good relation-ships to ensure that our job and life is made easier?

---

[1] Tom Peters and Robert Waterman. *In Search of Excellence: Lessons from America's Best Run Companies.* New York: Harper & Row, 1982.

How to you ensure good customer relations? I'm sure that many of you are familiar with the golden rule. I remember every year in Sunday school we discussed it: "Treat other people the way you want to be treated." Yet every day, I see others being rude, completely ignoring someone else and generally not following the golden rule.

Why would I deliberately treat someone poorly just because I don't have to work with them?

I joke about who our customers are. My company has many customers. My Purolator delivery man is my customer. And yes, I'm his too. I am nice to him—he is nice to me. Stephen Covey would call that a win-win situation. I want to ensure that my packages are delivered in good condition the next day. He wants to ensure that I keep using Purolator (job security you know). My family is my customer too. It is in my best interest that we have a good working relationship!

It just amazes me how many people just don't get this concept. Having a good, happy, enjoyable life is all about relation-ships! If you want good service in a store, restaurant, government office, or anywhere, the easiest way to get good service is to be a good customer. Being a good customer means you have to communicate your needs and wants. If you are on the other side of the counter, the easiest way to get good customers is to provide good service, and that involves, you guessed it, good communication. .

That doesn't sound like rocket science does it? Do me a favor—for the next seven days walk around with your ears focused on what you are hearing other people Are people treating others they way they want to be treated? Are you?

Red Light and Green Light Words

I've been spending a lot of time recently with Customer Service training, whether it is face-to-face or over the telephone. During that training we spend some time discussing how our customers interpret different words as well as the potential impact those words have. So what makes for good communication? There are some big picture things, like making sure that your attention is on the person you're talking to and not on the e-mail you're writing, or talking to the person, not at them, and in language they can understand. But there're also a lot of little things as well—and that's the stuff I want to concentrate on.

Let me use a traffic light analogy. When you are communicating with another person it is like there is a series of traffic lights between you both. If everything in that communication is positive and going well, it is a clear stream of green lights. Green means "Go." If either of the participants uses a "slightly" negative word, one of the lights turns amber. Perhaps their body language will put another amber light up. If enough amber lights appear, then some lights will go red. When too many of the lights go red, the communication breaks down and the customer will go away unhappy. Red means "Stop," and that's exactly what happens to the communication.

Some "green light" words are: *money saving, time saving, fast, simple...* words that help people. People like those type of words. Think about the commercials that we watch on television. Those types of words are used extensively throughout because they leave us with a positive impression. If we use positive words, we get green lights.

The "red light words" are a little easier to spot—which is probably a good thing because these are the ones we need to avoid. Words like: *can't, try, maybe, you have to, it's company policy, impossible, but…,* and the list could go on and on. You know how you feel when you are on the receiving end of those words. Do you really want to use them with your customers or co-workers?

So pay attention to the messages you are sending with those words. We all have heard the expression, "It's not what you say, it's how you say it," and while I will not disagree with that statement, it really is also what you say. In other words, keep your communications green.

CAN OR CAN'T?

There are obviously a ton of "red light" words, but the word that annoys me more than most is "can't." Have you ever analyzed what words you use and what they really mean? When teaching communication skills, I like to have a little bit of fun doing exactly that. I have a couple of pet peeves—and the word "can't" falls into that category.

What "can't" you do? You can do pretty much almost anything you want to do. Does can't mean "not able to" or "not willing to"?

When my kids were younger, there were certain words that were off limits in the house. We called them "swear" words. "Can't" was on the list.

As a parent, it would drive me crazy when my four-year-old would tell me, "I can't clean up the playroom." The same is true when a co-worker tells me that she "can't get that done in time."

My mind says, "Yes, you can. You just aren't willing to."

I had a participant in London, Ontario share with me that "I can't" is an acrostic of:

I

Certainly

Am

Not

Trying.

My son really could clean up the playroom, he just didn't want to. My co-worker really could get the document done in time, but she felt that something else was a priority and chose to do it first.

You really can: work overtime, stop everything you are doing and work on a project, get up in the morning, bungee jump, drive a hundred miles-an-hour, and so on. You choose not to!

Instead of telling people what you can't do, tell them what you can do. Why?

- It is a much more positive and assertive way to communicate.

- It makes you feel more in control of your actions.

- It is clear and concise.

The next time your instant response to a request is "I can't," think about what you can do, and offer that instead:

"Rhonda, can you please stop by the post office on the way home and mail this package?"

"Actually, I have an appointment that doesn't allow for stops. I can do that on Monday morning on the way to work if you like." Or...

"Can you stay and work on this tonight?"

"I need to leave the office by 5:00 p.m., but I can work on it first thing Monday morning when I get in."

"Can you bring the laundry up from the basement?"

"I'm not going downstairs right now, but when I do go later, I will gladly bring it up."

See how much more in control these responses sound? You will find that you receive less opposition (less red light reaction) and are seen as an assertive communicator when you talk about what you can do rather than what you can't.

I DON'T KNOW

Sometimes, though, there are words or phrases that are tough to call—red? Or green? Here's one of my favorite examples. For Christmas last year, I found one of those "Page a Day" calendars— "For Women Who Do Too Much," under the tree. My husband thought this gift was not only appropriate, but very funny, too! Apparently, he thinks I try to do too much! Anyway, one of the pages stood out a little more than the others:

> *The most difficult words in the English language*
> *(and the most powerful!) are:*
> ### *"I don't know."*

So here's a tough question: Is it okay to say to a client (internal or external), a co-worker, *anybody* really, "I don't know"?

This question always gets everyone sitting on the edge of their seats in my Customer Service workshops. Many of my participants think that, no, it's not okay because it makes it look like you don't know what you are doing, and you could lose credibility. Can't disagree with that.

Others think that this is just fine to say, "Sorry, I don't know," and let the customer figure out another option for getting the information. If they knew the information they would share it. Better to be honest than to tell the customer a lie, right?

I think that there is a happy medium. Yes, it is fine to say, "I don't know" as long as that isn't the entire statement. Follow it up with, "But I will find out immediately and get back to you in ten minutes," or something along those lines. We have to be sure that the information that follows the "I don't know" is helpful, though.

A few years ago I was in Midwestern state, staying in one of those areas that you would really rather not stay in—but it was close to the client and relatively moderately priced. It was also one of those "hotels" that did not have interior corridors and outside access only—in other words, it was a motel. When I was checking in, I had parked my car (under a light) near the front the hotel. Of course, the room I was given was about as far away from the front of the hotel as you could get—and there was no parking at that end of the hotel. (Are you getting the picture? I was not too comfortable). I asked the desk clerk if there was anywhere to park closer to that room. Her response: "I don't know; I never go to the back of the hotel." With that, she walked away.

This is exactly what I'm talking about when I get on my soapbox about good customer communication. You know, she could have handled that a whole lot better. I can understand that she has never been back there—but I'm sure that someone in the hotel has been and could have been called. Perhaps saying, "I don't know because I've never actually been to the back of the hotel. I know that someone in maintenance will know, and I can call them right now for you," would have made me feel a lot better.

So, while common practice says it's fine not to know the answer, common sense says it's not fine to let the sentence stop there.

The upshot? Keep your communications green light friendly by just paying attention to your word choice—you will be amazed at the results!

If You Want My Advice...
Too Bad!

Well, as I put this together, I think this is turning into something of a "what not to do in a communication situation" chapter. But maybe that's not such a bad thing. We all know what good communication looks like. I want to help you through all those times when you, or someone else, is threatening the flow of communication.

This one is all about giving advice. Now, I have to tell you, I have a very fragile ego. I know it, and freely admit it.

I get my feelings hurt easily, and although I, ironically, teach "Dealing with Difficult People" and "Confrontation Skills," I prefer not to do either if I don't have to.

Recently, someone gave me some unsolicited advice, and it really bothered me.

I was delivering my "Amazing Assistant" program to a client, and everything was flowing smoothly. The participants were having a really good time, and I was thoroughly enjoying myself, knowing the client, the firm's training co-ordinator, would be very happy with the results.

At lunch I planned to sit with a group of participants to enjoy the social part of the day. When I went to see if the training co-ordinator would like to join us, I was greeted with: "I have some feedback to give you about your training program. I see some ways you can make it better."

Since I hadn't asked for the advice, it threw me for a loop. Unfortunately, I took it the wrong way and proceeded to second-guess myself the entire afternoon.

While I was processing how I felt about this unsolicited advice, I realized that I am an advice-giver by trade, and that I had potentially done the same thing to others: annoying them with unasked-for suggestions.

I wondered how many other people do the same thing. We may be simply trying to make a task easier for someone or to show them a different way to do something. But if we weren't asked for this advice, why do we assume the other person will be open to receiving it?

When you say to someone (your children, for instance), "Here, let me help you with that," are you giving advice that hasn't been asked for?

The next time you question someone ("Why did you do it that way?" or "That seems like a difficult way to..." or "that's not the way we do it here") you run the risk that your advice will not be received in a positive manner.

Offering this kind of advice potentially sets up barriers to good working relationships with people. It can also have a cumulative effect, fostering a negative perception of you over time.

I know that the training coordinator had my best interests at heart. I know she wasn't telling me that I wasn't doing a good job. That didn't stop me from resenting the unsolicited advice.

It is easy to come across as a know-it-all and be one of those difficult people I've been teaching everyone to deal with. It is easy to come across as a busybody, with nothing better to do than tell others what they do wrong. It is very easy to send the wrong message with good intentions.

For the next thirty days, join me in an experiment I practice often. I'm going to try not to offer any unsolicited advice. I'm going to simply keep quiet. My motto is, if someone wants advice, they will ask and in the meantime I won't assume they want it.

After the thirty days of "no advice" are over, try following this handy checklist that I always use now before I offer up advice:

- Is the other person looking for advice? Is she open to it and willing to hear it?

- Is my comment kind? Or, is my intention to point out that the person is doing something wrong? What is my intent?

- Will the other person feel good about receiving it? Does it make me look like I know better than they do? Is this about me?

- Is this the right time to give this advice?

Based on the answers, we may decide to keep the advice to ourselves after all…at least until someone asks for it.

Do You Interrupt Others?

Knock, knock! Who's there?

Interrupting cow.

Interrupting cow wh—MOOOOO!

(Please pause for this interruption.)

I admit I have a very bad habit that is incredibly annoying. Okay, so I have many annoying habits. But I'll just talk about one here: I cut people off when they're speaking.

I don't intend to be rude. I just seem to think that I know where the other person is going and that I can get there faster. I get so caught up in what I want to say that I stop listening and start sharing my own thoughts. Selfish, isn't it? It's also condescending. It sends this message to the other person: "What you are saying isn't nearly as important as what I want to say."

I blame my interrupting habit on my family. I grew up next door to my grandparents, and I have a large extended family. When I was a kid, I'd march through the cow field and have dinner at Granny's. As anyone in a large family knows, when you're eating dinner with a lot of other family members, table manners tend to disappear—out of necessity. If there's only one dinner roll on the table, you'd better grab it before anyone notices. You wouldn't think of asking anyone else if they wanted it—because you would likely never get it yourself.

Conversation was much the same way. If you happened to be quiet during dinner, no one noticed you were not speaking and no one would ask you what was bothering you. If you had something you wanted to share with everyone, you needed to speak up, speak quickly, and speak louder than everyone else.

But just because I've been communicating this way my entire life doesn't make it right! Regardless of how I learned the habit of interrupting others, I do need to break it, because it's disrespectful, rude, and unprofessional. I've been working a long time on breaking this bad habit. I'm willing to bet that many other people are trying to break this habit as well.

Here are some tips that I'm using, practically everyday sometimes, to help myself not interrupt. I trust you will find them helpful:

CATCH YOURSELF

Be aware when you cut someone off. Stop your sentence midstream, and apologize for being rude. This will take discipline on your part to interrupt yourself once you've caught yourself in the act

ASK FOR HELP FROM YOUR LOVED ONES

They are the best ones to ask for help, as they will be very happy to point out your mistakes. Ask them to kindly point out when you've cut them off so you can be more aware of how often you do it.

PLACE A SIGN ON YOUR PHONE

Or at your desk, that says "Be *Nice*" (or has some other positive message). Post the sign in several locations throughout your workspace as well as in your home. It sounds childish, but the more you remind yourself (in a positive way) to stop interrupting others, the more likely you are to stop interrupting others.

REWARD YOURSELF

Count how many times a day you interrupt others. Set a goal in the morning along the lines of: "If I interrupt others less than ten times today, I will stop at Starbucks on the way home from work." Continue to lower the goal daily until you can get to the point where you are not interrupting anyone.

Learn to bite your tongue. Literally. I make a point to hold my tongue in my mouth until the person is finished speaking (and believe me sometimes that takes effort!). This takes conscious effort because my lips often move without my brain being in gear. (Does anyone else have this problem?). Wait, breathe, wait and then respond when it is clear they are finished speaking. It takes lots of practice, but your friends, co-workers, family members and clients will appreciate the effort.

Even if you're worried that you'll forget what you were going to say if you wait until the other person is finished speaking, bite your tongue. And, if you do forget what you were going to say in the next thirty seconds, it probably wasn't all that important anyway. It doesn't matter what your reasons are for interrupting others; you and I both need to learn to break this bad and annoying habit. It stops communication cold. Not good.

You Can Stop Awfulizing
(and prevent others from doing it to you)

Many people make things worse than they are and create a sense of panic before there is anything to worry about. These people imagine how awful circumstances can be; and then they worry about it, usually out loud. So while I'm on a "what not to say" kick, I have to address this other pet peeve of mine.

There is actually a new word for what these people are doing, and it makes perfect sense:

> **Awfulize** v. to imagine or predict the worst
> circumstances or outcome.
> Source: www.doubletongued.org

My husband Warren and I spent one New Year's Eve in New York City. We were traveling home on January first, and while we were checking out of the hotel, I asked the desk clerk to please call us a taxi to the airport. The look on her face had me concerned immediately. She told us that this was a holiday, and that taxis don't work on holidays. She then said it would be a very long wait to find one to take us to the airport.

Now, as a professional speaker, I travel extensively, and in my experience, taxis do not have "'no-work days," especially in a city like New York with a couple of million tourists there for the big countdown. I calmly smiled, and asked her to call anyway. In the meantime, Warren walked outside the hotel and flagged down a taxi within the first minute.

I wonder if a less experienced traveler would have fallen victim to the clerk's awfulizing? It seems to have become more and more a common practice—and I can understand (if not agree) with that. Awfulizing can be incredibly contagious. Here are some examples.

AWFULIZING THE WEATHER

One week in early January, I was off to California for a speaking engagement. My mother called me the day before I was to leave to see if the airports were still open. Apparently California was getting quite a lot of rain and they were concerned about mud slides. Okay, that's a legitimate concern—for some. But my mom— she began awfulizing about it. I told my mom that even if there were mud slides, the airport would still be open. Rain does not stop air travel (especially to southern California in January).

I remained calm again, and that allowed me to not catch the awfulizing virus she was trying to share (albeit unconsciously).

AWFULIZING AT WORK

How about awfulizing at the office? Do you remember the last time you were told that your department was getting a new manager? Did a group of people get together and imagine what type of ogre she was going to be?

Statistically, two out of three people don't like their job. Why they stay puzzles me, but one reason people stay is that they awfulize about the new job they imagine. They haven't even applied for another job, but they spend time making the worst of a new situation (that hasn't even happened yet!) and avoid even looking for that new job because it might be as terrible as they imagine.

Why do we do that? More importantly, how can we stop this bad habit immediately?

Here are some tips to help keep your cool, and to avoid awfulizing or being awfulized:

Stay Calm

This is how I handled my mom. I remained calm and that allowed me to not catch the awfulizing virus.

Smile, and say to yourself, "I'm not going there." No matter what the situation: when the weatherman tells you that we are in for a major snowstorm; as you prepare for a meeting or a family gathering, even with people you don't know well; at work when you have a staff meeting, or a downsizing, or a new boss on the way, take that deep breath, and instead of awfulizing, affirm something positive. "Great! The flowers really need a natural watering. We'll get more moisture in this storm." Or "I'm going to rock that presentation." When you stay calm, you're better able to turn the negative awfulizing into something positive.

Put everything into perspective

I avoid awfulizing the unknown by putting it into perspective.

Ask yourself: what is the current situation? What is the worst possible situation, and what is the best possible situation? Once you've established the range, look at the most likely situation. Putting everything into perspective allows you to look at (and potentially prepare for) the worst-case scenario, but it will also help you to see that it is not likely to happen. The new boss might be horrible; she may have no management experience and micromanage you. Or, maybe she's perfect for you and you'll end up loving your job and your boss. Reality says that the truth is probably somewhere in the middle. If it is as horrible as you awfulized it, you can get a new job. If it is as perfect as you would like, then you'll be really happy. Either way, you still can do something to be happy about your new situation instead of worrying that you'll have a terrible new boss.

Focus on the "right now" rather than the future

Getting caught up in future consequences is classic awfulizing. Stay with the now, and not the future. Worrying about your new boss, or that you'll get demoted or fired, is not about the here and now, it's awfulizing about the future. Worry about now and then revert back to tip number two: Put everything into perspective.

Avoid "absolute thinking" such as "always" and "never"

"We'll never get a taxi in New York City on New Year's Day," is awfulizing. Even if it was true, it would be better, and more accurate, to say, "It will be difficult to get a taxi in New York City on New Year's Day."

Find humor in the situation

When you're able to laugh at something by finding the humor in it, then it's much easier to use humor and find something positive about even the worst situation. Make light of the fact that you get to spend extra time in an amazing place like New York if you really can't find that taxi. Joke that your new boss will be like the ones on *The Office* or *Mary Tyler Moore*. It's hard to awfulize when you're laughing.

Awfulizing is a bad habit that is completely within your control to change. Don't worry about what you can't change, and change what you can.

How Do You Handle Compliments?

"A compliment is a gift, not to be thrown away carelessly unless you want to hurt the giver."
Ziff Davis

Here's a biggie that women, especially, have some trouble with. Has anyone ever said to you as you walk into the office "Hey, you look nice today"? What did you respond with?

Many of us think "'Oh sure—what do you want?'" or "'What did I look like yesterday?'" Sound familiar? For most of us it does because we are uncomfortable with compliments.

Statistically, two out of three adults suffer from low self-esteem and low self-confidence.[2] Doesn't that seem amazingly high to you? Two-thirds of the population are unsure of themselves.

Now don't get me wrong, they may not be unsure of themselves in every aspect of their life—but certainly in some.

I will admit that my appearance is one area I'm not as confident as I should be (this is not your cue to compliment how I look either —but thanks for the thought). When someone tells me I look nice, I feel an overwhelming urge to move that compliment to an area where I do have high self-confidence. That area is my ability to shop! I am a professional shopper. There are days when I think that I single handedly keep the economy going! So, if someone tells me that I look nice, I tell them what a great deal I got on the

---

[2] Jack Canfield. *How to Build Your High Self-Esteem*. Nightingale Conant Corp, 1989.

suit, or how much I paid for it! For some reason, I'm comfortable with compliments on my ability to shop.

Yet, if you refer to the quote I started with—I am unintentionally insulting my friend. Do I mean to hurt them? No. Just because I need to work on my self-confidence doesn't mean that my friends need to pay the price for it.

So here's another project that you can take up in the months that follow: for the next month (it takes twenty-one to twenty-eight days to start to create a habit), whenever (and every time!) someone gives you a compliment, say "thank you." End of sentence, period, no more unless it is appropriate. Don't throw away their kindness—unless of course you want to hurt the giver. (I didn't think so).

Do You Sound Credible?

It is too easy to focus on what we do wrong, and very difficult to focus on what we do right. I don't want to seem like I'm giving negative advice all the time. (Common sense says to be positive right?) I could go on and on about what not to do in a communication situation. But I want to switch gears here. In a work situation, common sense also says to be professional at all times. Part of a professional demeanor is sounding credible, and credibility comes from both the words you use and how you use them.

One way to get the idea of what I'm talking about is to watch all the *Law & Order* types of shows that seem to be on television every night. I've been particularly drawn to them of late. I like to pretend I am the investigator; I pay close attention to the suspects. I have found that sometimes they are very credible in what they say and how they say it. Those people are usually the good guys. Now, yes, I realize these are TV shows and the people aren't real. However, they still give us insight into what people say and the way that they say it—and whether or not we believe what they are saying.

Credibility makes such a difference. It can make a lot of good things happen in your life, such as job promotions and job security. Lack of credibility, on the other hand, can hurt your reputation and cost you those same promotions or potentially your job.

YOU'RE IN CONTROL

Credibility is one of those invisible skills that we have quite a bit of control over. It can affect every aspect of your life including your professional life. Luckily, there are many ways in which you can control your credibility.

First, let's assume you are not going to be interviewed by any police officers in the near future. Rather let's talk about what happens at work. Listen to yourself the next time you are in a meeting to detect whether you get yourself into trouble with any of the following credibility crunchers.

Using absolutes: When you use words like "always" and "never," you are using absolutes. You will probably lose some credibility by using absolutes. It almost sounds like a child having a temper tantrum: "You never take me to McDonald's!"—something that isn't, in fact, true. Using absolutes can make the receiver become defensive. It tends to put barriers (or a "red light") into the conversation; you end up not listening properly and, without realizing it, you can begin to sound aggressive.

Not using forceful words: Words that are monosyllabic (have one syllable) are the most forceful words in the English language. Think about some of the great speeches of our time:

> *"Ask not what your country can do for you,*
> *but what you can do for your country…"*

John F. Kennedy, January 20, 1961,
at his inauguration in Washington, DC

Or

> *"I have a dream…"*

Dr. Martin Luther King—August 28, 1963,
in Washington, DC

This is powerful stuff, and most of it is said with one-syllable words. Don't confuse the issue with big, fancy words. Professional communication skills require that the person you are speaking to understand the meaning of the words you are using. Using fancy words from the darkest depths of the dictionary can make your message sound aggressive, or at least pompous. Simple, one-syllable words are easy to understand, easy to remember, and have an assertive, powerful feeling to them.

Overusing junk words or trendy phrases: We all have favorite phrases that we use over and over again. Often we aren't even aware that we're using—and overusing—them. But you can be sure that the person who works in the cubicle next to you knows exactly what yours are, in the same way that you know what theirs are. A great example of a repetitive, junk word is "uh" in every sentence. With "uh," most of the time the speaker is unaware she has used it. It becomes a vocal habit.

Many people use "okay" to transition from one thought to the next, as well as "um" or "ah". Many trendy phrases such as "yadda-yadda" (from Seinfeld), or "24-7" tend to be used repetitively. You will find that some people use these types of phrases excessively, even in situations in which they don't apply. The danger is the appearance or flavor they give your message. They're usually not the types of things you hear from CEOs or senior level managers (or at least, they shouldn't be heard at that level). These types of habits take away our credibility.

Here's a list of other trendy words that you want to use sparingly:

Synergy: This one popped up in the early '90s and hasn't disappeared. It seems that we must have synergy in everything we do! The next time you bring a group of people to work on a project, don't tell them it's because there is better synergy. Tell them that we work better together.

Framework: Trendy phrases have appropriate use and inappropriate use. If framework is the appropriate phrase, it is fine to use it sparingly. But avoid asking people to give you the framework of a situation. That usage isn't appropriate.

Ballpark: Not the Blue Jays or Yankees kind of ballpark, but a "'ballpark" figure. It is a trendy way to say that the person is approximating or even guessing. When someone tells me she is giving me a ballpark figure, I will assume it isn't correct, that it will be an estimate. If a plumber were to give me a ballpark figure on what it would cost to fix my plumbing, I would be skeptical of that figure, and assume a higher one would be more accurate.

Bottom line: Some people use this phrase as if they owned it. They will interrupt you mid-sentence and ask you to get to the bottom line. This phrase is useful when reviewing financial statements, but if your co-worker is telling you about a problem he is experiencing, there is no bottom line. Use "bottom line" if you want the bottom line of a financial report; otherwise, remove this trendy phrase from your lexicon.

Think outside the box: Another one that has been around for more than a decade. It would give you more credibility to use a different expression, or a different way to describe what you are looking for.

The problem with overusing these types of phrases is the loss of credibility you immediately receive. As soon as you utter your favorite overused phrase, others will (invisibly) roll their eyes and tune you out.

To keep our listeners in tune with our message, we need to be aware of the traps we fall into. Trendy phrases represent a minor trap, and one which is easily fixed. By removing them, you elevate your credibility and keep your listener tuned in to what you are saying.

NOT PAUSING OR OVER-PAUSING

Pausing can have great impact on your message as well, in both a positive and negative sense. If you pause too much, it looks like you don't know what you are going to say, and you lose impact. But pausing appropriately can make you seem very deliberate and strategic in your use of words and, therefore, lend you some credib-ility. Rushing through your words with few pauses, on the other hand, can make you sound scatter-brained, overly excitable, and wound-up like a top.

So where is the perfect balance? In the one-two dance step. Any place in a sentence where there would normally be a comma, a semi-colon, a period or other punctuation, say to yourself one-two (at the same speed as a waltz dance step: speak one-two, speak one-two) .

There are so many things that can take away our credibility. Fortunately, there are many things we can do to increase our credibility. What you say and how you say it is always up to you.

A few years ago, I attended an amazing conference designed to build my business. The facilitator was an extremely successful businessman from Florida. He was amazed at the words we chose to use to describe our businesses, our success, and our dreams. He pointed out to us that we took away our own power, prestige, and positioning by what we chose to say. We were crunching our own credibility, and we weren't even aware of it! Once he started to bring it to our attention, we became more conscious of it. Sure, we blamed the entire thing on the Canadian lack of boastful pride that, perhaps, we all have. Our facilitator indicated that this mistake was not only Canadian, it had a worldwide impact and we needed to be aware that we were hurting ourselves by speaking that way.

I hear the following "softening phrases" being used in many countries—not just Canada—and by both sexes. I've even said them myself. What we need to be aware of is how these words are affecting the image other people have of us.

SOFTENING PHRASES

Softening phrases work against us, especially when we aren't in charge. Without even realizing it, they take away our credibility. They make us appear far more passive than we realize. This causes others to assume we are not competent or professional. Just by changing a few simple words you can improve your image. What is one of the biggest softening words? Try.

Try is closely associated with the word "can't". We use the word, *try*, when we aren't sure of what we can or can't do. For instance: someone comes up to your desk and asks if you can get report "A" done for 5:00 p.m. You are swamped with work, but you really like the person and want to help her, so you say, "I'll try." In your own mind you are saying, "I really doubt that I can help you, but because I don't know what else to say, I'll tell you I'll try to get it done. But don't expect that it will get done." The other person heard, "It will be done."

This is a classic communication error. Don't tell people what you'll try to do—tell them what you will do. Use an assertive, confident tone and tell them what you will do. That way, you won't be seen or treated as passive and subsequently lose the respect of your co-worker.

I'M SORRY

Another softening phrase is, "I'm sorry." We use the phrase to be polite. The problem is that the words are perceived as taking responsibility. If you could have avoided the situation and you chose not to, then "I'm sorry" is appropriate. It is not appropriate to say "I'm sorry" when you are bumped into by another person, when you are asking someone to repeat what she said, or when you can not do what the other person wants you to do.

Take, for example, the situation in which you are working at your desk and a supervisor comes up to you and asks you to take care of an item for her. Assume you are really busy working on a number-one priority task and are unable to help her. Should you say, "I'm sorry, I can't help you right now"? Only if you really are sorry, which in many cases, you probably are not. If you really are disappointed, upset and genuinely sorry, then say you're sorry. Otherwise, you are using the wrong words.

The higher up the corporate ladder people climb, the less likely they are to use the words "I'm sorry." Be aware of your use of this phrase. When you are sorry, be sure to say you are sorry. When you are just being polite, choose other words. For instance, if someone asks you to attend a meeting for them, instead of saying "I'm sorry, I can't go today," be polite and say "Thank you for asking me. I am unable to attend."

I WISH

The words "I wish" are also softening words, because they give the impression that you don't know what you can or cannot do. This gives the appearance of passivity. People who are assertive or even aggressive are very clear on what they can do and cannot do so they wouldn't use the words, "I wish."

I give you this list not to make you wrong if you say these phrases. We all use these phrases at one time or another. I just want to point out that it is amazing how often we crunch our own credibility just by using certain soft words and phrases or by saying them in the wrong way. Fortunately, it can easily be avoided by taking a more critical look at the things we say and the way we say them. Be proud of what you know. Speak firmly, confidently, and with passion, and you will automatically appear more credible—and that can only help you in any communication situation!

Voice Mail
Tips to Guarantee a Positive Impression

I would be remiss to not talk about another very important communication situation—one that is here to stay, no matter if you like it or not, and one that threatens to turn people off even before you've actually had a chance to speak to him or her personally. Yep, like the title says, it's voice mail. Voice mail is an argument that has people on both sides of the fence. Some people love it while others hate it! For my Canadian readers, I'm sure they'll remember back a few years ago when a major Canadian city had all voice mail removed. These city officials had their reasons and at the time they made sense.

The arguments against voice mail are many: the personal touch is removed, customer service should be delivered by a person, no one ever returns voice mail, and so on. Those people on the positive side of voice mail will tell you that it helps them manage their time better, helps them service the client better and is a positive addition to the tools available to the employee today. I personally can argue on both sides of the equation and in the end, it doesn't really matter. Voice mail is here to stay! If that is the case, let's use it to our advantage! But let's also use some common sense…

Here are my tips for good voice-mail practices:

RECORDING A MESSAGE

- Limit your personal greeting to thirty seconds; make sure your voice is businesslike but cheerful. Try to not to make your message too long. You would be surprised at how long thirty seconds is. You can say quite a bit in that time. If you deliver your greeting in multiple languages (let's use English and French since that's pretty typical up north here in Canada) after the end of the first language delivery, tell your client that they can press the pound key (#) to skip the rest of the message. This way they don't need to listen to the message again in another language. For multiple language greetings, be sure that they are as short as possible.

- Keep your clients and customers in mind when recording your greeting, specifically where language is concerned. For instance, I live in Ottawa, which is a completely bilingual city (French & English). Most people either speak both languages or understand both languages. It is quite common to call an office and hear a bilingual greeting. Unfortunately, if their client base is not entirely in the Ottawa area, it is possible that their client does not understand the entire message.

Here's an example of a message I hear frequently: Example: "Hello, you have reached the office of Jane Smith. *Je ne suis pas disponible maintenant.* Please leave your name and number and I will return your call by the end of the business day."

If I am calling from Chicago, I may not have understood the middle section of your message and I may have hung up. At the very least, it isn't good customer service. It is also an example of what not to do on voice mail.

- Keep your personal greeting current. I am a big believer that everyone should change their voice mail greeting daily. It shows to your customer that you at least check it once a day! It gives me the confidence that you are attentive to the telephone area of your job. If I have that confidence, I won't call you three times that day, just once (which saves you time, doesn't it?). Now please, don't forget to update it! There is nothing worse than calling and hearing a date that is three weeks old! This is definitely not a good impression of you and your company!

- List no more than three or four options, one of which should always be to reach a live operator. Make sure that you list the option before the number they should press as well. For instance: "If you wish to speak to a live representative, press zero." That sounds much better than: "Press zero to speak to a live operator." I tend not to listen closely to the options until I hear the one I want. If the number I should press was mentioned before the option, I may not have heard what it was. I know this sounds silly, but the next time you are given options, pay attention to how closely you listen to the numbers.

Here's an example of a typical message on my phone:

"This is Rhonda Scharf of the Training Department of ON THE RIGHT TRACK - Training & Consulting. Today is Monday, May 12, 2009, and I will be out of the office in the morning and able to return calls after 1:00 p.m. this afternoon. In the meantime, please leave your name and telephone number including area code, your organization, a complete message and the best time to return your call. I'll be sure to call you back before the end of the business day."

This message took twenty seconds for me to leave. Oh, and make sure that you manage your voice mail by not only recording a good message but checking them regularly as well!

VOICE MAIL REMINDERS

- When leaving the office (even just for lunch), forward calls to your voice mail system. Don't have the phone ring three times if you aren't there. You are wasting your customer's time!

- When away from the office for several days or more, leave the name and number of someone who can help in your absence. If people jump to the end of your message without evening listening to it, have someone else record your greeting when you are away from the office. This will avoid you returning to the office with your message box full!

- Don't hide behind voice mail, return messages promptly.

Voice mail is often the first time a customer or client will have any contact with your company. It kind of goes back to the Golden Rule I mentioned earlier—treat others as you yourself would like to be treated. Leave a voice mail that you, yourself, would find helpful, and you'll get your communication off On-The-Right-Track!

Frustrated?
Don't Call Me!

Okay, while we're on the subject of automated messages, I have to tell you about something that happened to me that I'll never forget. It kind of took everything I've just told you not to do and put it all into one long nightmare of an experience. It was so bad, so frustrating, that I really felt paralyzed, not knowing what I should do next. Have you ever been in that kind of situation?

While it was happening, I also felt angry and scared. I also felt extremely stupid because I didn't know what else I should be doing since what I had been doing hadn't gotten me anywhere.

It all started quite innocently really. I decided to change my phone system from a standard phone line to the new digital voice, or VOIP (Voice over Internet Protocol). This was going to make my life so much easier because my phone number would be permanent for life. Regardless of where I was in North America, my clients could call my main business line and I would answer. My phone—a decent one, not the poor-reception-quality cell phone variety—would travel with me.

I would also have one phone number for life. Quite a brilliant little trick the phone company came up with, or so I thought when I first heard about it. When I attempted to change to VOIP, I had just experienced a couple of years filled with change for me, my kids, my friends, and my clients. I had recently moved, which required a new phone number and address. I changed my name, another huge change. And then I moved again. It was starting to look like I was deliberately trying to lose my clients. I did not want another phone number.

So I called the phone company to get everything digital, and (most importantly) consistent. "Absolutely," they told me, and initially everything was On-The-Right-Track and flowing smoothly. I was quite proud of my solution and ingenuity, that is until the nightmare started happening...

First, they disconnected my main business line. My clients wondered what had happened to me. Of course, my toll-free number and fax numbers, which are also associated with that phone number, weren't working either. I spent about four hours a day on my cell phone with the phone company trying to find out what had happened and get everything working again. I started to panic, assuming I was losing business by the minute.

On the outside, however, I stayed cool. I accepted transfers and lengthy on-hold times with professionalism. I kept track of every phone number, every name, every ticket number and date I was given. I explained, many, many times, my frustration over losing contact with the world through my telephone, and my concern that it appeared to be something they could not fix. Nonetheless, I must have given off a negative vibe during a phone call because just four days later, my VOIP phone number was cancelled...disconnected...permanently.

This left me completely without phone access in or out of my office.

The first three times, I was told that my problem would be fixed by 7:00 p.m. that night. I gladly got off my cell phone (it was a huge bill that month!), pleased that my ability to clearly communicate had prevailed, and I congratulated myself on having made myself understood. Little did I know....

Over the next week, I think I spent virtually every waking hour on the phone with the phone company trying to get my business out of the virtual trash bin, to bring my heart rate down to a normal rate, and to slow down the graying hair and wrinkling process my frustration level had accelerated.

My frustration was overwhelming me twenty-four hours a day. I am a good, clear, concise communicator. After all, I am a specialist in communications, yet I hit a brick wall at every turn.

But I kept trying. I clearly explained what was happening, to each of the one-hundred-plus employees at Bell with whom I spoke. I was sure they understood what I needed, and why I was so frustrated. (In defense of Bell employees, about 95 percent of them were fantastic. They seemed to care about my situation, and wanted to get me up and running again as quickly as possible. It's that other five percent that turned my hair gray.)

I was transferred a lot. In my customer service training programs, I talk about the importance of doing a live transfer instead of just sending the caller off alone in another direction. This experience solidified my perspective on this, and for those few at Bell who did live transfers, thank you so much, because they do make a difference.

Throughout this process, I learned how exasperating it is for the customer to deal with a large organization that has many specialties. Much of what I felt stemmed from having been sent from department to department because each person had their own individual specialty and I needed to deal with, seemingly, all of them. My challenge was that each time I was transferred to yet another division, it felt like I was starting all over again. As you can imagine, I was tearing my hair out, not to mention losing valuable production time because it was incredibly frustrating and time consuming.

At one point, we even had to start the entire process from scratch because my history had been "cancelled" and what I was guaranteed to have happen would in fact not be happening.

In the end, I did indeed have a new phone number for clients. However, Siame at Bell has given me a back-door solution as well. I also have multiple phone numbers clients can access me through, one of them being my former office number. I didn't want my clients to lose me through my life-and-phone-number transitions.

I eventually had to give up on VOIP. However, the silver lining is that experience will provide terrific fodder for a great module in some of my future training programs. At the end of the day, I am not forever sworn off the phone company. For a long time after we came up with a workable solution, I remained frustrated and fearful that the solution we came up with would not work the way I needed it to. I was afraid I would lose customers in the transition. What is amazing to me is how long I remained paralyzed in fear that the awful experience would repeat itself endlessly. Then, I finally realized I was "awfulizing" the situation. I took a deep breath, realized it was all over and then vowed never to change my phone number again! And I haven't.

It took everything I knew about good communication to keep my cool throughout this whole process. I also realize that good communication happens not between a person and a computer or a person and a faceless system, but between people—and the best kind of communication happens when both parties are willing to participate.

Are You Listening?

There's one final component to good communication that I want to address before I move on to other topics. I've spent a good number of pages telling you what to say and what not to say, but this is really more of a skill that we all need to develop—the art of listening.

There is a big difference between hearing and listening. Your teenage kids, they hear you...they just aren't listening! Many times we do exactly the same thing. Listening means much more than hearing. We all have some pretty bad habits. Unfortunately, many good communication situations break down because the person receiving the communication just isn't listening. It's become, unfortunately, a very bad habit for many. I've found that there are a number of reasons why people don't listen. Here are my top four:

- The number one poor listening habit (which 90 percent of us of do) is *interrupting*! I've already had my say on this one—since I'm just as guilty as all the rest on this bad habit—so for some good tips on how to not interrupt people and listen to them instead, see "Do You Interrupt Others?"

- The second bad habit on our listening list is the "Fear of not having all the answers." This tends to happen to us (at work) when we are new in the job. Everyone seems to hate saying "I don't know" so we listen just long enough to get an answer in our head. The problem is, it often isn't the answer to the question.

For example: you call into a company and tell the receptionist that you would like to speak to Ms. Jones. Now before you are even finished, the receptionist says, "She isn't in right now. Would you like to leave a message?" The problem is that you weren't finished asking your question because the receptionist didn't hear the part about: "In person, next week at her convenience." Not only did she interrupt, she wanted to have an answer to your question. She answered the wrong question.

- Over-reacting. Oops, I'm guilty again! There are some situations that I chronically over-react in. We all have "hot-buttons." We just need anyone to push them—and boom! We're gone!

Another example that happens to me almost every weekend: On Saturday night in my house, we watch *Hockey Night in Canada* (what else eh?). Between the first and second period, CBC has a time slot for none other than Don Cherry. Now Mr. Cherry is extremely good at his job—so good in fact that I will over-react to everything he has to say! Why? Because I don't listen. I over-react. We often have people in our offices and personal lives that we just don't listen to. They know exactly where our hot buttons are and just love to push them.

- The final bad listening habit is "Pseudo listening." Basically, this means "pretending to listen." Anyone who is married has done this (oops, I'm guilty again!) But, are you doing it at work, with clients, with co-workers, or heaven forbid, your boss? Be sure to catch yourself when you are "pretending." The clue for you are the "uh huh's" we say over and over again.

I know that if you think about these bad habits, you too will confess a little guilt. Are you interesting in creating good listening habits?

I am pretty sure that you will find if you focus on your listening just a little bit, you will find fewer misunderstandings.

Good communication isn't that hard, really, if we start paying attention to what we're saying and to what others are saying to us. Unfortunately, common practice has helped us develop some bad communication habits. Maybe it's because we're constantly bombarded with information that we don't know who and what to respond to, so we've given up. Perhaps it's because we've become lazy. Whatever it is, I think we tend to forget nowadays that we're actually talking *to* someone instead of *at* them.

Common sense always has good manners attached to it. Slow down. Think about what you're saying and how your communication is being received. Make sure to actively listen to what's being said to you, and you'll find that you are communicating well.

PART THREE

How to Make Nice in the Sandbox: The Importance of Teamwork in the Workplace

It's the stuff we learned in kindergarten. Play nice. Share. There's a whole list of things Robert Fulghum told us over twenty years ago in *All I Need to Know I Learned in Kindergarten*, and they were spot on. Unfortunately, some of the kids didn't learn the rules back then, and they certainly don't use them now. What it comes down to is teamwork—in other words how to work together toward a common goal. Current common practice is that we tend to think of ourselves as mere cogs in a giant corporate wheel. We do what's listed on our job description, and assume we're doing a good job. There's no sense of team spirit in that mentality, and that's a problem. Common sense says, no matter what position you hold in an organization, there're some fundamental aspects of teamwork that are essential for you to know to be a success in your organization. In other words, make sure that you know the basic rules of playing nice in the sandbox at work.

The Sense of a Goose

Every year in the fall I look enviously at the geese flying south for the winter. Canadian winters are fine, but I'm sure that I could really tolerate the sun and the beach all winter, too. The other day I was watching them fly, remembering the analogy that I use in my Team Building workshops.

As you look up, you will see the geese flying in a "V" shape. Did you ever wonder why? Well, as each bird flaps its wings, it will create an uplift for the bird immediately following. By flying in formation, the whole flock adds at least 71 percent greater flying range than if each bird flew alone. Pretty easy to create a Team Building analogy here isn't it? We are far more powerful when we work as a team and benefit from the uplift the other team members are creating. People who share a common direction and sense of community can get where they are going more quickly and easily because they are traveling on the thrust of one another. This applies in pretty much all settings—corporate, small business, even in a family. The better we work as a collective group or team, the more we can accomplish.

But there's something else that happens with these geese. When one goose falls out of formation, it suddenly feels the drag and resistance of trying to go it alone. It quickly gets back into formation to take advantage of the lifting power of the bird in front. When you feel the drag of falling out of formation, look to get back in with the rest of the flock. Most of us complain a little about having to do everything ourselves, but don't look to get back together with the others. If you are working too hard, you are probably flying alone.

When the head goose gets tired, it rotates back in the wing and another goose flies point. It is sensible to take turns doing demanding jobs, whether with people at work, in the family, or with geese flying south.

Geese honk from behind to encourage those up front to keep up their speed. What messages do we give when we honk from behind?

Finally, and this is important, when a goose gets sick or is wounded by a gunshot, and falls out of formation, two other geese fall out with that goose and follow it down to lend help and protection. They stay with the fallen goose until it is able to fly or until it dies, and only then do they launch out on their own, or with another formation to catch up with their group.

I don't think I need to belabour the obvious—just think about this: geese, in a way, are the ultimate team.

The Common Commitment

Now, the "why" of what I just said—that geese are the ultimate team—isn't as obvious as the fact that they are a team, and that's what I want to take up here. What really lies at the heart of a good team?

We've probably all heard the expression "There is no 'I' in Team!" Yet really, what does that mean? I've been spending some time with several different companies and helping them get to a "performing stage" of teamwork. Yet, I've noticed a common problem with all these teams.

Teamwork really is defined as a group of people who collaborate and interact to reach a common goal. The problem is that common goal. Everyone seems to have a different interpretation of what that common goal is.

If you were to think about the five most important tasks that sit on your desk from day to day—what would they be? Ask you supervisor (or supervisors) the very same question. This is important. I'm willing to bet that your list and your supervisor's list would be considerably different.

How can we be working as a team (even if it is only a team of two) if we are working toward different goals?

This different goal problem not only affects teamwork, it also affects time management, priority management, stress management and communication! Hard to believe that such a little tiny detail can have such a big impact.

Back in the early 1990's, the popular trend in corporations was defining the Mission Statement. I can count on one hand how many people have their Mission Statement memorized. I usually advise my clients to go down to the front lobby of their office, and they will find it on hanging in a beautiful frame on the wall. Mission Statements were a great idea—the follow through was the problem.

As companies, departments, teams and workgroups we need to know what our individual team goal is. Perhaps it is the same as the one in the front lobby—whether that is Customer Service, High Quality or Cost Effectiveness. But goals that make a team cohere are usually also more fine-tuned than those lofty aspirations. In order to make your team work well in your particular sandbox, you need to find out what you're all working toward—what is your common commitment that makes the group gel.

If you don't know, my recommendation is to have a meeting with your team (go ahead and organize it yourself, your supervisors will be glad you did, trust me) to find out what that "Common Commitment" really is. Not only will you look good, your entire team will benefit from the results. But—here's the kicker—do more than just talk about it, follow through. Find ways to make that commitment happen in real time. You *will* be pleased with the results!

Taking Initiative

You know, I think one of the biggest dangers of working in an office is becoming complacent. It goes back to just following your job description, making sure your work gets done, and calling it a day. I've worked in an office environment long enough to know that this is common practice.

When I'm training in organizations I make it a point to speak to several "higher-up" people within the company to ensure that I'm delivering a consistent message to the message the attendees have been receiving in the past. To do this, I ask many questions. One of them is "What would you like your employees to be able to do that they are not currently doing?" I get a variety of answers, but one of the most common is "I'd like them to take more initiative in the office—and do things without being asked."

Have you ever received a comment like that on a performance evaluation? I have—and it frustrated me. What could I do differently? I was doing what I was supposed to do. The key word in their answer, however, is the key not only to a better performance evaluation but to being a better teammate in general. The word: initiative.

First, let's start with a definition. *Initiative* is defined as "the action of taking the first step or move; the ability to think and act without being urged." Since somewhere in the early 1990's this has been referred to as being "proactive." Whatever you call it, we need to be proactive in our jobs (do things before they need to be done) instead of reactive (doing things after the need has been identified) in order to forward the goals of the team.

Now, let's take a moment and think about why we hold back and are not proactive or don't take the initiative. Sometimes they are simple reasons like "I just don't have time to do anything extra"; or realistic like "If I do it once—then it becomes my job" (think cleaning the fridge at work!). Other reasons that keep us from taking initiate: fear that others may think we are overstepping our boundaries and are acting "too big for our shoes"; fear that it may look like we don't have enough work to do and we are looking for more; if you're a perfectionist like me, we don't want to do something new for fear of not doing it correctly. Perhaps we have "learned" not to do anything extra as it doesn't get you anything (or does it?) hmmmmm.

I teach people to stop looking at all the negative reasons why we don't take the initiative and start looking at the positive side of acting without being asked to. (Think of your own kids here and how you convince them to do things before you ask them to!). The following is a list of suggestions I make in my workshops. I hope you find them helpful:

Question: *When do you take the initiative to make decisions?*

Answer: *When you know what needs to be done.*

If you know the answer to a question or are able to fix a problem, why are you waiting? I get soooo frustrated when I find a note on the counter that says, "We need milk." Don't you just want to scream? Or how about when your teenager or spouse tells you the car needs gas! Sure, these aren't office examples, but you get my point. If you know what needs to be done—*and it follows the other two guidelines below*—just do it! You're right. No one will probably notice (at first), but over time your initiative will start to become apparent to the person you are helping out. It takes time, but the payoffs are potentially enormous.

TAKE INITIATIVE WHEN IT IS IN YOUR REALM OF AUTHORITY

Now I have to be honest here, this is where I used to trip myself up short. When you see something that must be done, and you are fully willing and capable of doing it, you have to ask yourself: what is your realm of authority? This is the tricky part. If you have been in your position for a few years, your authority expands as you gain the trust and confidence of others that you work with. If you are new to your position, your realm of authority is pretty limited. If the task you want to undertake is mentioned in your job description; that is totally safe. If not, you have to use judgment (back to the common sense theory). Know that you also "push" your realm of authority in little steps. If it is "just" beyond a decision that you recently made you are probably fine to make this decision as well. If you are wrong and it was not in your realm of authority, you will be told! (Learned that yet?). The tricky part is to expand your realm of authority in little steps. If you took a little step over the line (or past a recent decision) it likely won't cost you your job. If you take a flying leap over that line, you might be looking for a new job.

TAKE INITIATIVE WHEN IT IS SUPPORTING THE TEAM

You see something that needs to be done. You're not sure if you're overstepping your boundaries. Here are some additional guidelines to make the right decision: are you saving the team extra work? Would it take more time and effort to pass it onto someone else? If another member of your team is swamped with work, and you are in a position to save them time by making a decision or doing something for them, do it! The person you helped will be grateful and your team will be happy that they're moving toward the goal. Common sense right? Is it your practice?

I believe that what goes around comes around. Yes, it may seem like extra work for you to take initiative. But remember this: people work well with people who are easy to work with.

Make yourself that person, and you'll always get picked to be on a winning team!

Begin With the End in Mind

Have you ever asked someone to do something for you, and you were disappointed with the results? I have! When I look back at the original request, everything seems quite clear to me, yet in the end, it is obviously not.

Teamwork can be frustrating as well as rewarding. You know what you want, but you can't do it yourself. You need help, but you want it done right. How do you proceed? The problem is, some people have different working styles as well as different working standards. This is where we run into problems when we work with others, and common practice has been to just deal with the problem. Instead, when you need to enlist someone's help, take Stephen Covey's advice and let the person do the job in his or her own way.

Stephen Covey, for those of you who aren't familiar with him, wrote a very influential business book called *The Seven Habits of Highly Effective People*. One of the most quoted "habits" is all about "beginning with the end in mind."[3] Basically, that means to begin with the final picture. As you are handing over a task, ask yourself, what does the end product need to look like? Then describe what you want to happen in a visual manner so the person who is going to do your job can "see" what you are hoping to accomplish.

Now this is all fine and well you say, but often, the project goes all wrong because the person failed to see the steps to get to the final picture. But let's look at this problem. Is this yours—or theirs?

---

3 Stephen Covey. *The Seven Habits of Highly Effective People*. New York: Free Press, 2004 (1989).

Let me tell you a story about me when I was growing up. We lived in the country, and while I love to make exaggerated jokes about me growing up in the sticks, a very real thing that we did do was use the clothes line to dry our clothes—twelve months of the year! Yes, we had a dryer, but Mom preferred the clothes line (that nice smell, you know). Well, one very, very cold Ottawa winter day (and you know how cold it can get in Canada!), Mom asked me to hang the clothes out on the line. I hated hanging clothes out in the winter. Not only were your fingers in danger of severe frostbite, I hated it when I brought my Levi's in from outside and I could stand them up in the corner, not because they were stiff but because they were frozen! So, like all kids, I put up the token fuss. She didn't listen of course. She just marched me outside, hamper in hand.

Now here's the problem: my mom had a certain way that clothes needed to be hung up to dry. You were to hang the shirts with the shirts (upside down, too), the pants with the pants (matched at the seams, upside down), the underwear all together, and socks paired and hung together. According to Mom, "this is the way it must be done."

On this particular day I was more concerned with getting the clothes on the line before all my fingers fell off. So what did I do? I hung them up in any order just to get them hung on the line. After all, that is what I was asked to do, right?

When I came back into the house, Mom gave me one of those "mom" looks and asked how I could be finished so quickly. Then she turned and looked out the window at the clothes line. At that point she lost it! According to her, I did it all wrong.

My point in this argument was that she asked me to hang the clothes on the line. The final result should be that the clothes come back in the house dry. That is how I interpreted those instructions. So when the clothes that I hung up come back in was she going to be able to tell that her pants were dried between two pieces of Dad's underwear? No. The final result was what she wanted—dry clothes.

She was very clear on the final result she wanted. Does it matter how they got that way? In this case the answer is no. She also didn't tell me why she wanted them hung up in that certain order—it made the folding and putting away part of the chore much easier. If she had, I might have complied—or not. It *was* really cold that day.

Now let's bring this back to the work place. Let's say the task is answering the phone. In this situation, how that task gets done might very well matter. Let's say you're my employee. To be professional, I tell you that the phone needs to be answered by the second ring, and it needs to be answered by saying, "ABC Company, Rhonda speaking. How may I help you?"

If I were to ask you to answer the phone, is that clear enough? Knowing that people have different work styles and standards, the answer would be "No, that isn't enough." I know this because those were the exact instructions I gave my sons one day when I had to leave my home office and they happened to be home. My boys don't like to answer the phone, but Christopher, who was eleven at the time, grumblingly agreed. Guess how he answered the phone: "Hello, who is this?" Not exactly what I had in mind. I didn't tell him why he needed to be more professional with his greeting. It was partially my fault, though, not entirely his.

So when you need someone to do something, begin with the end in mind. Don't worry about the details *unless they affect the end result.* If that's the case, then be prepared to offer the details, and explain to them why it must be done that particular way. If the details aren't essential, the person might ask for them anyway. It might just save them time, but if it's not important, respect them if they don't want your details.

The next time you ask someone to copy and collate some workbooks for you, be clear on what that end result is. If the result is really to just get the workbooks put together, does it matter how the copying gets done?

We Can Learn a lot from The Apprentice Or, Whom Do You Trust?

I like reality television. I love to watch the interactions between the contestants. I am particularly fond of *The Apprentice* because it shows people in professional situations.

What I find fascinating is that the contestants seem genuinely surprised when they have trusted someone only to find that they shouldn't have. Don't they realize that it is everyone for himself or herself? Even though there are "teams," in the end, only one person wins the prize and the others don't want it to be you.

Unfortunately, our work settings are often similar to reality TV. Sometimes we trust people we shouldn't trust, and we get burned. But, in order to have an effective team, we have to be able to trust that our teammates are at least pulling their weight. So where's the happy middle?

Don't get me wrong, the people you work with are probably wonderful people. But like reality television, they are at work to further their own careers and reputations, not yours. They will not offer themselves as a sacrifice so you can get ahead. It just isn't going to happen.

So here are some tips to keep you "in the game" of today's reality workplace.

COLLEAGUES ARE NOT TRUE FRIENDS

Work is not the place to find a spouse or a best friend. The people you work with are the people you work with. You have in common anything that happens between 9 a.m. and 5 p.m., but little outside of that. Your kids may be the same age, but they probably don't go to the same school. You may like to do the same things, you may even play on a baseball team together, but ultimately what you have in common is your workplace. Don't lose sight of that. Don't be as open with them as you are with your "real friends."

I've had people with whom I worked become friends in my personal life, only to find out that I never should have made that crossover. What happens if one of you is promoted to be the supervisor of the other? What happens if one of you has to fire the other? What happens if you start dating? The credibility of both people suffers in those situations. You can't win. You will feel as if the other person has stabbed you in the back (or vice-versa). You can be friendly; you can chat a little about your personal life, but don't be booking a trip to Florida with a professional colleague. The pain of the metaphoric knife in the back is severe.

BUSINESS PREVAILS OVER FRIENDSHIP

Your colleagues may be friendly at work. However, if they need to, they will turn against you the very same way that people do on reality television. Don't fool yourself into thinking they would fall on their sword for you, they won't. Don't assume that your definition of friendship is the same as theirs. Think reality television.

Here's a true anecdote about a betrayal that happened to me at work. I often don't tell clients that I am based in Ottawa because quite a few of them are in Toronto. Many times I will not charge extra for travel. This way, I can't be edged out because I'm not local. I recently had a professional colleague/friend use the fact that I wasn't a local speaker to win out a client. The client didn't know where I was based, and it really didn't matter. But my colleague used this information to his advantage, and I lost out professionally. He knew that the client didn't know where I was based, he knew my strategy about not revealing that, and he used it to his advantage. I was hurt, because I wasn't realistic about the parameters of our friendship. I assumed that friendship would prevail over business.

Wrong.

ETHICS SHOULD ALWAYS PREVAIL OVER BUSINESS

Someone once shared with me that she would "test" co-workers to see which ones she could trust or not. She would give them a tidbit of information and see if it got passed on. If it was, she knew exactly where it came from.

It is not acceptable to stab a co-worker in the back. Just because someone is a work colleague rather than a friend doesn't mean ethics fly out the window. Use your own good judgment in all matters, including business. Don't use information to your advantage just because you can. If you wouldn't want someone to use inside knowledge against you professionally, be sure that you are not doing it either.

KNOW THE DIFFERENCE BETWEEN HONESTY AND TOTAL HONESTY

Have you ever been forced to tell the whole truth knowing that if you did, someone would get hurt? There is a difference between honesty and total honesty. Honesty is acting with integrity.

It is always telling the truth, not ever telling a lie, but not always telling the whole picture either. For example, if someone comes into the office wearing what you consider to be a dreadful tie and shirt combination, and they ask, "Do you like my tie?" You could respond, "Yes." You aren't lying, you like the tie, just not with that shirt. Total honesty would be, "The shirt and tie combination is dreadful." Since the combination wasn't what the person asked you about, you are not telling a lie. You are being honest with integrity, just not totally honest.

If tomorrow you are tired because you were fighting with your teenaged daughter all evening and someone asks, "Why are you so tired? Didn't you sleep last night?" You can honestly reply, "I spent the night thinking and couldn't sleep," which is true. You don't have to say you were thinking about the fact that your teen-aged daughter is becoming a vampire. This is information that can be used against you. Besides, that information isn't needed for you to be honest.

BE SELECTIVE ABOUT WHAT YOU SHARE WITH CO-WORKERS

If it comes down to one promotion, the other person will do what she needs to do to get that promotion. That may mean working to undermine your credibility or even to share something personal about you that may negatively affect the perspective of the person hiring. Perhaps your colleague will use the fact that your mother is very ill and suggest that is affecting your concentration. Maybe you and your spouse are having challenges. When everything in the friendship is going well, it is easy to share everything that is happening in your personal life. Please be careful. When my marriage was falling apart, I told very few people. I was selective about who I told because I didn't want anyone to think that it affected the way I did my job.

Trust is something you will have with a select few people. It is unrealistic to think that most of the people you should trust are at work. Be worthy of the trust that others have placed in you, and be selective of those in whom you place your trust. There are few things that hurt as much as being betrayed by someone you considered a friend. By understanding the difference between work colleagues and true friends, you will be setting realistic expectations for yourself, rather than setting yourself up for a fall.

Procrastination...
Don't Create Dis-ease
with this Disease!

When you're working in a team, one way to ensure your colleagues won't trust you is to not do what you say you're going to do. Common sense tells us that, but we rationalize our actions by believing that procrastination is acceptable. Common practice is not common sense either.

Procrastination feels good at the time. It definitely gets you out of doing things that you really don't want to do. So the purpose of procrastination is good, but it always seems to add more stress and disorganization to our lives, and it certainly doesn't foster good will in our teammates.

But instead of telling you that it's not okay, let's look at ways you can avoid it. Can you recognize when you are procrastinating? Do you know what to do when you catch yourself?

Procrastination is like creating a snowball on the top of a mountain. For a little while, it is just fine. If you move the snowball around too much up there, it takes on a life of its own and travels down the mountain on its own steam. We know that it crashes when it hits bottom! Have you ever done that? I have, and I would like to be better about not doing it again.

We start the cycle by saying, "I'll do that tomorrow," or "I will be more focused to do that tomorrow," or even, "I don't have the energy to do that today." Those are not bad statements—until tomorrow comes and we say the same thing.

Here's my rule, if you have procrastinated three times in a row, you have a problem. So how do you get over it? First, start by recognizing when you have procrastinated. Be totally honest with yourself and say, "Yes—I really am putting this off—and I really don't have a good reason." That is half the battle.

Then, choose one of the following techniques and stick with it until you get the task done:

TELL SOMEONE ELSE THAT YOU ARE COMMITTED TO GETTING IT DONE

Make an out-loud commitment to someone else. Make that someone be a person that will make you keep your word, that won't take your excuses or explanations. Your dog doesn't count!

GIVE YOURSELF A DEADLINE

Many of us truly believe that we work better under pressure. Sometimes we really do. Therefore, those things that don't have deadlines (or the deadlines are very far into the future), we just never seem to get around to. So say, "I will have three pages of this report written by next Tuesday," and hold yourself to that deadline.

BREAK THE TASK INTO LITTLE PIECES

Some people prefer to start with the easy tasks to keep the momentum going and some people like to start with the hard tasks to get them out of the way. The way to figure out your style is quite simple. When you were a child and you had a vegetable on your plate that you hated—but you *had* to eat it—when did you eat the vegetable? If you ate it first, then you should start with the difficult task first. If you ate the vegetable last, then start with the easy parts of the task. If you mixed it up into the potatoes to hide the taste, you need to just start anywhere and get going. Finally, if you gave your vegetable to the dog, you should probably delegate the task!

BE SURE TO KEEP THE TASK FRONT AND CENTER ON YOUR DESK

If you put it in the filing cabinet, it is very easy to forget about it. By keeping the task front and centre on your desk, it is almost like nagging yourself. If it is always staring you in the face, it is hard to keep procrastinating. I do this with the ironing in my house. To be honest, I iron everything. I know that isn't necessary, but once I get going with my ironing, I quite enjoy it. So I leave the ironing board up in the family room with all the clothes piled in a basket beside it. When I'm in the living room, I will usually get up and iron once I see the pile growing!

DON'T WAIT UNTIL THE LAST MINUTE

I know we work better under pressure, but get some of it done before it is too late! This way you won't have your snowball take off down the mountain without you!

I keep this little rhyme in my head and remind myself that the pain of procrastination is not worth the small reward we get when we do procrastinate:

> *Procrastination is my sin*
> *It gives me pain and sorrow*
> *But I can stop most anytime,*
> *I think I'll change tomorrow!*

There are times when procrastination brings about good results. And that might be fine if you are the only one involved. But your procrastination can drive your teammates nuts. It can make them angry, and next thing you know, there's a fight in the sandbox. That's what we're trying to avoid here—so try to avoid…avoiding your task. Everyone will be more productive because of it.

Solution or Band-Aid?

I began this section on teamwork talking about the importance of having a common goal. I'm going to end it with the idea that we work towards achieving those goals by being able to solve the problems that get in our way.

According to Tom Peters, in *In Search of Excellence,* 86 percent of all business problems can be solved by the people actually doing the job[4]—isn't that what a team is all about?

The challenge we face in problem solving is we first tend to assume we know what the problem is, and then we are quick to put a corporate "band-aid" on these misdiagnosed problems. What we need to focus on is understanding what the problem is before we rush off to find a solution.

Voice mail is one example of a corporate "band-aid." I've talked about voice mail and how to use it correctly, but what made voice mail so attractive in the first place? The first assumed problem was that people weren't at their telephones and are therefore not able to answer their telephones. Solution: employ a receptionist just to take messages. Approximate salary for a receptionist: $15,000 – $25,000 (early 1990s, prior-to-voice-mail price) a year.

And then voice mail was introduced. Assumed problem: "we're spending too much money for someone to just take messages." Solution: voice mail. Companies embraced the solution and

---

[4] Tom Peters and Robert Waterman. *In Search of Excellence: Lessons from America's Best Run Companies.* New York: Harper & Row, 1982.

promptly spent more than the receptionist's salary on equipment and training to implement it. Did it work? Or did it create a multitude of additional problems?

Of course the answer is that for many companies it was a costly, time-consuming "new problem" that became worse than the original "problem." The situation is a classic red flag, signifying that perhaps the original problem was incorrectly defined right from the start.

To help understand a problem fully and then find the best solution, the following questions need to be asked:

HOW BIG IS THE PROBLEM?

Is it something that can be solved immediately (or in the very-short-term)? Might other people or resources need to be involved? (Be careful about adding more people to solve the problem.) The common assumption is that the more people who are involved, the more widespread the ownership, and the higher the likelihood the solution will prove successful.

WHY IS IT A PROBLEM?

This key question helps with the "understanding" component of problem solving. In the voice mail example, the why was assumed to be financial. The receptionist was costing money, so the problem appeared to be a financial one.

I don't believe that was the problem at all. Perhaps the problem was an issue of customer service, expectations, or commitment. Answering the telephone is more than a voice mail problem. The voice mail solution created more of a problem because 'not answering the phone' was never the real "why" at all.

WHAT ARE THE CONSEQUENCES OF DOING NOTHING?

Looking at the consequences of doing nothing may push you into making a decision now, deferring it, or even ignoring the problem altogether. Corporate business has looked at the voice mail problem in a couple of different ways. Some companies have created "Service Level Agreements" with their customers stating that they will return all calls within *x* timeframe, thereby focusing on the real issue of expectations and customer service. Other companies chose to remove voice mail altogether. Most companies chose to ignore the problem completely and behave as if voice mail is the solution to the original "assumed" problem.

What does a successful solution look like? How will we know whether we've got the right solution or we've put a band-aid on it? If we spent time, effort and money on solving the problem, what would the measurable outcome be? Have we saved the money a receptionist cost us? No, and in the end many more dollars are wasted playing voice mail tag and listening to a dozen three-minute voice mail messages every day.

Teamwork involves being able to handle challenges. If the challenge in your workplace is the misdiagnosis of problems, be sure to review these three points. You may find that your "solution" is more of a "band-aid."

In teamwork we are working with more than one person, and the dangers of not following common sense multiply exponentially. The little things become big things. By the same token, the little successes can easily become big successes as well. Teams must create "team common sense" ground rules to ensure their success whether that is through follow through guidelines, initiative expectations for each member, confidentiality rules or just plain respect. Organiza-tion, communication and common sense and your team will be On-The-Right-Track to bigger and better things!

PART FOUR

Life and Work: A Juggling Act or a Balancing Ballet?

We spend an enormous amount of our time at work. But is "work" our "life"? I think the answer is yes and no. *Yes*, because it is so much a part of our waking hours. *No*, because there is so much more to life than work. Our work-a-day world, for one reason or another, is threatening more and more to take over our entire lives. It is also seemingly more and more okay to bring life into work and work into life. Life happens. Work also happens. What follows is some common sense wisdom I've offered my clients over the years on the entire work/life balance struggle. It's not the be-all-and-end-all answer to where you draw the line. That's up to you. I just hope this gets you thinking about where you place your line.

Do You Bring Your Work Home with You— or Your Family to Work

When you've had a bad day at work, and your temper is short, and you have no patience left—do you bring it home with you?

Absolutely, unequivocally, unfortunately, I know the answer is "yes." Because we all do it every once in a while; it's inevitable. The key is to limit the amount of cross-over between work and life, to achieve a healthy balance that works for everyone, including ourselves, our family, and our colleagues.

When I was growing up, my dad came home every night precisely at 4:45 p.m. Dinner was at five. I knew what my dad said he did for a living, but other than the title, I didn't know what it was that he actually did, or even where he did it. I never heard my dad complain about his workload, his boss, or the environment at work. I never, ever heard my dad say anything negative about what he did for a living.

On the other hand, when my mom went back to work full-time when I was twelve, I knew what she did and where she worked. I not only knew her co-workers and boss by name, but I even babysat for them. I knew when my mom had had a bad day or a good one.

I was an adult before I understood that both approaches have good points and bad points, and that there is a workable middle-ground between the two.

Work takes up a huge portion of our waking time. It is natural that we sometimes bring some of our work-life home. In fact, I believe it is important to share that part of your life with your family. They should understand when you have had a bad day, and when you have something to celebrate. (There's also the flipside to this scenario. If you have some stress happening at home, it isn't necessarily important to always share that with your co-workers. While it's fine to treat some of your closest work colleagues as friends, it becomes a problem when it starts to interfere with your work.)

I used to work with a group of women that I considered friends as well as co-workers. We were like giggly high-school girls at lunch. We shared our lives together—our troubles, our joys, the good and the bad, but the bad started to outweigh the good fairly quickly. Our lunchtimes became bitch sessions, and it was affecting my work. Soon, I began avoiding our lunchtime gatherings.

Of course, co-workers can be fairly easily avoided. Family cannot. Does your family want to avoid you when you come home? Are you bringing home your negativity, your bad moods and frustrations and taking them out on the family?

DO YOURSELF AND YOUR FAMILY A FAVOR, AND GIVE YOURSELF A FEW RULES TO FOLLOW:

1. Tell your family members when you've had a bad day, but don't feel the need to elaborate. It's okay to tell them you are frustrated, or are even in a bad mood, but it isn't right to take your frustrations out on them.

2. Don't use a bad day as an excuse for bad behavior. Having a bad day is never a justification to behave badly towards your family (or anyone for that matter).

3. Your family should be your port in a storm. Keep it that way by treating them as the special people they are in your life. Show them you are glad to be home.

4. When you see your front door, remind yourself you are happy to be home. Tell yourself that what happened at work is over now, and that you are going to walk away from it. Then, walk away from it.

(If you find that you're one of the people who brings her family frustrations to the office, you can follow these same rules—simply swap the words "work" and "home.")

We are all human. We all make mistakes and we will all take out our anger on the wrong person every once in a while. However, with a little effort and a little awareness, we can separate our "two lives" and not ask our loved ones to take the blame for things that happened at work.

Work Less, Live More

I once had an affair…with my job. It started around 2001 and wasn't just for a few busy weeks either, it went on for a couple of years. I cheated on my husband and my children, spending a significant amount of time away from them. I cheated them out of time they should have had with their wife and mother.

My "partner" was available twenty-four hours a day, seven days a week. "He" was easy to spend time with…and was fun and rewarding. He was at the end of a phone call, at the keyboard of my computer, and anywhere, any time I wanted. I had full access to my affair. And, over time, I became not only addicted, but obsessive. I worked all the time. I was always thinking about work, doing work, and spending time in my office. This obsession fed my self-esteem and my own identification. I was lost without something to do. I thought I was happiest when I was working. I was making things happen.

As with a real affair, the consequences were huge. The cost was very high, my marriage for one, time lost with my kids for another. When the affair ended, I didn't know what to do with myself. I didn't know how to spend my time. I was lost in my own world.

My family paid the price for this affair, the same way they would have had the affair actually been with a person. I spent time with my job instead of my husband or children. I preferred my office to the family room.

Even on vacations I was in contact with my job. I could check my e-mail any time, check my voice mail, and just touch base with a client every now and again. I justified it by telling myself if I did all that during a vacation, I could write the vacation off on my taxes! I read the newspaper thinking about my clients. I surfed the 'net to find out what was new in my industry. I was in love with what I did and it occupied my mind completely.

Does this sound familiar to you? Whether you are self-employed or not, it is so incredibly easy to have an affair with your job. Technology virtually assures that you can stay in touch with work non-stop. BlackBerrys, cell phones, e-mail, portable computers, WiFi everywhere...what are we setting ourselves up for?

If, like me, you have difficulties with this issue, I would like to challenge you to change your priorities. Your work will not suffer if you step back a little. My business is actually more successful now than when I was having an affair. I was so obsessed with what I was doing, I was working hard but not smart. Now that I ration the time in my office and with my job, I have to work smart, because I am unwilling to ever pay this kind of price again.

If you don't have to check your work e-mail from your home, then don't. It will still be there in the morning. If you can't do anything about the voice mail that comes in after hours, don't even listen to it. It will occupy your mind in the evening, causing you to mentally remove yourself from your family.

Plan to work eight hours a day. That's all you get paid for, so why work eighteen? Learn to work smart, not just hard. Read a book, take a course, or listen to a CD on working smarter, not harder. Stop assuming that not only is this normal, that it is okay to do it. It is not.

Cut back on the hours you work from home, even if it's by just thirty minutes a day. When you close the door to your home-office, keep the door closed. Lock it. Put a sign on the door that says "Spending time with my family. Will return in the morning."

We are all familiar with the "imagine your own funeral" routine. People do not talk about how great you were because you worked all the time, but what you accomplished in your personal life.

If you really are someone who needs to be busy all the time, be busy with your family. Volunteer at a soup kitchen or at the local women's shelter. Visit the elderly in a nursing home (and while you're there, ask them if they wish they had worked less). Spend time with friends and family.

I love my job. I would be lost without it. But I could replace it with something else. My life is a one-shot deal. I can't replace it. I can't replace my kids either. Don't gamble with your life so you can answer your e-mail or risk your relationship so you can spend more time at the office.

Treasure the gifts you've been given, and take care of them.

Are You Prone to STRESS?

Stress, Stress, Stress. Why are we so stressed? What is different now than compared to forty years ago? *Everything* is the answer. Take a look at your weekly schedule. Is there any extra time just for you? Or, are you like most people, and have virtually every moment accounted for—working, doing something for, or with, someone else?

When I teach my Stress Management programs, I never cease to be amazed at the levels of stress that people are under. And many of them function quite well at those astronomical levels. But only for a while.

The problem of not having a good work/life ratio is that is causes stress. It is quite possible that you could be pushing your body beyond its limits. And that can cause all sorts of problems— physically and mentally. I really want you to be productive and happy, as well as successful, in your work and in your life. So, I'm going to give you the same test I give my workshop participants to find out if they are susceptible in responding to stress. Answer the following questions as honestly as you can:

- Are you over-scheduled? Do you take on more than you can do? Are you unable to say no, and therefore have no time of your own? Do you over-commit?

- Are you a perfectionist? Do you try to be the perfect employee, lover, wife, husband, mother, father, daughter, son, sister, brother, and aunt or uncle? Are you always hard on yourself and feel you could have done better?

- Do you worry about what people will think? Do you go over how you looked, acted, sounded? Do you rerun conversations in your head? Do you wake up in the middle of the night and say, "Oh, I should have said…"?

- Do you hate to wait? Do you have difficulty waiting—for a co-worker to finish a report, at the photocopier, in line at the bank, grocery store, department store, traffic jams, waiting for friends to show up?

- Are you a constant worrier?

- Are you unable to take time for yourself? Do you need constant stimulation? Can you take silence? Do you need the television, radio or something else playing in the background?

If you answered "yes" to two or more of these questions, chances are that stress has become a way of life for you.

Now that you have identified that you are prone (or not), do something about it *before* your body does something for you—and that's the subject of the next piece….

A Facelift for the Mind
Reduce Negative Stress

It doesn't seem to matter your age, your sex, your position in life or how much money you make. Stress is a fact of life. The causes of stress are slightly different for each of us, but it still exists. And it can be dangerous. If you read the paper, every once in a while you find that stress will kill us if we don't learn how to handle it!

Now, before I go any further, not all stress is bad! There is such a thing as positive stress, and we need a little bit of that every so often. For those of you (and I'm one of them) who really believe that you do your best work under pressure (also sometimes referred to as procrastination—see the previous section); know that when you work that way, you are creating your own stress—even though it can be "good" stress, it still can be harmful if it happens too often.

So, let us focus on what kind of stress to get rid of—and how to do it.

NEGATIVE STRESSORS IN YOUR LIFE

Worry

Do you worry about the things that you can change, or worry about things that you can't? Negative stress comes from worrying about things that you have no power to change. It would be a bit ridiculous of me to tell you to stop worrying about those things (like weather). So what you need to do is ask yourself "What can I do to make the worry go away (or feel better)?" and focus your energy in that direction. I recognize that sometimes we worry about things that we can't do anything about, so try to channel your worry into something productive. I can't do anything about freezing rain, but I can put salt on my walk to make sure that no one falls.

No Clear Meaning or Purpose

A common question for adults is, "What do you want to do when you grow up?" People laugh, but they have no idea! Not having a purpose can cause stress, even debilitating depression. Goal setting will help make this very negative energy and stress into positive energy and stress. For example, stop getting stressed about hating your job—find out what you want to do instead. At first you may not be able to do what it is that you want, but at least your energy is focused.

Unfinished Business

Did you stop your education before it was finished? For how many years have you been saying, "Someday I'm going to go back and finish my degree, or get my MBA?" Either make the plans and do something about it—or decide that you will never do anything about it and stop causing yourself negative stress about it.

Unresolved Conflict

Pick up the phone and apologize to that friend or co-worker you've had words with. This is the kind of negative stress that keeps me up at night. Which is worse: telling someone you're sorry that it happened, or killing yourself from not saying anything? Agree that the subject will never be brought up again, that there will be no blame cast on either side, and that you are sorry that the entire mess ever happened.

Fear of Failure

Ah…We've all heard this one before, yet we still continue to fall victim to the negative stress it creates. Think of the things we won't or don't do because we are afraid of what people might say, of what they might think, and that perhaps we might fail. The fear of public speaking is the number one fear of all people. When I am teaching my presentation skills course, nerves are a big topic! Many people are petrified of speaking in front of a group. Why? Because they might forget what they were trying to say, might say something really stupid, and might look bad in front of their peers. Bottom line, they are afraid of failing.

Now, I must admit, that is a pretty fair fear. I'm afraid of failing too. And because of that, it creates negative stress. How do you handle that? Instead of denying yourself the opportunity to try something that you might not fail at—figure out all the things that can go wrong. Then, plan for them. If you fail to plan, you plan to fail! Excuse the cliché, but it's 100 percent true. Yes, we might fail. But what might we lose if we don't even try? Instead of brewing over the negative effects of whatever it is you are holding yourself back from—do it! Plan it! Succeed! You'll never learn how if you don't try.

Fear of Rejection

Another very valid stress. I have a great amount of compassion for the young adults that take jobs as telephone solicitors whose job it is to call us at dinnertime. The rejection rate must be extremely high. I hear many people laugh about how they said no to the person on the other end of the phone. While their responses are humorous, the person who called still faces rejection. Remember the days back in high school when you really wanted to ask someone out but were afraid to (just in case they said no)? Remember the stress that caused? That still happens when we want to ask for a raise, ask for time off, or a special request. My uncle just asked for a raise—for the first time ever! He got 10 percent!! Not bad. So I asked him why he waited so long to ask for something he felt he deserved. He was afraid to. The same rules for fear of rejection apply to fear of failure. They are very closely related. Plan what you want—go in prepared and just try! The number one problem in the sales cycle is asking for the sale. Why? Fear of rejection. What have you got to lose? You likely won't be fired for asking, especially if you are prepared.

Go for it!

Denial

This example is for those of you who hate your job—and have hated it for a while now. How long have you been kidding yourself about it getting better? People live in denial about their jobs, their relationships and their financial situations. Do you ever say, "It'll get better. Just give it time"? While I don't disagree with that statement, are you doing anything to make it better, or just waiting? Living in denial is refusing to see what is plain to anyone else. And refusing to do anything about it.

Anger

Being angry at someone or something can cause an enormous amount of stress. We're a culture that believes in holding your temper and not doing anything proactive about your anger. That can cause stress. But letting it all out can also be detrimental. Because anger can be so damaging to our mental health, here are some tips at handling anger so that it doesn't lead to more stress in your life:

- Keep logs of your anger: what makes you angry, who makes you angry and to whom you express it, your anger's duration, and any thoughts that accompany it.

- Deal with your anger directly. If possible, confront the person with whom you are angry, rather than taking it out on someone else or complaining about it to another person.

- Take several deep breaths and relax your muscles

- Exercise after work.

- Don't brood about what makes you angry. It only keeps you in a stress response and can lead to health problems.

- Ask yourself, "Is it worth getting upset about?" If it is, deal with it.

Things that upset you or stress you don't just disappear. We cannot ignore those events that are causing us stress—they will not go away.

All in all, *you have choices in life.* Sometimes, the most stress is caused by doing nothing about what is stressing you out. So, go ahead, make a choice. There are three main ones as I see it. You can:

- accept the way it is (and let go of the stress)

- change the situation (do something about it)

- leave the situation (quit or leave all together).

We know that we need to manage our stress. To lead healthier, happier lives, we need to learn to take advantage of the energy that positive stress creates and reduce the impact the negative stress generates. We need to identify where that negative stress is coming from. Do yourself, your family and your job a favor—reduce your negative stress. Your health and relationships will be improved. It really is a facelift for the mind!

If you apply all the techniques listed above, you have a lot of work on, and a lot to work with. It is worth the effort. Good Luck!

Let's Get Busy Doing Nothing!

One of the biggest stressors in life today, I think, is that we're too busy. It seems we are a culture of people who try to "out-busy" each other.

"Hi Rhonda. How are you today?"

"Busy. You know how it is. How about you?"

"Busy busy. It never stops!" And on the discussion goes.

When I was growing up, my brother and I attended church and Sunday school. I also attended Brownies or Girl Guides during the school year, and in the summer I played competitive baseball. My brother also went to church, and he played hockey and baseball.

That meant we were busy two or three days a week. All the other days were spent doing what kids did in the '70s and '80s—hanging out and having fun.

What are kids doing these days? I know that the adage is to keep them busy all the time so you know what they're up to. However, are we creating a society of kids who don't know how to relax? Are we teaching busy-making habits to our children and further reinforcing that being busy all the time is good?

Think about your plans for tonight. Do you plan on sitting on your back deck with a beverage trying to see how many birdcalls you can recognize? What about watching a sunset—when was the last time you did that? We all work hard. Some of us work too hard. Statistics tell us that about two-thirds of employees eat lunch at their desk each day. You need to get a break from work during the day. Even if you are on Facebook, YouTube, or DealingWithDifficultPeople.org while you are eating, your brain is still at work. Get away from your desk.

I'm a non-smoker. Always have been. However, there is a habit that smokers have that we non-smokers need to learn: to take a break. Your brain needs the break from being constantly surrounded by work. Even if your conscious mind is not working, your sub-conscious mind still is.

The BlackBerry/Palm Pilot may add to the problem. Turn it off. Don't look at it when you get home at night. Do something that is relaxing for you, something that isn't considered "busy work."

Here are some ideas to help you be "less busy" this week:

- Take a break at lunchtime today, even if you just spend fifteen minutes walking around your building. In the winter, we will be willing to pay money to get to the climate we get for free in the summer. Enjoy it whether it is hot or cold right now. Get outside.

- Tonight, make a point to get outside and watch the sunset. Walk around your yard, or your building, and look at the flowers. If they are your flowers, cut some (or go buy some) and put them in your kitchen or family room. If flowers aren't your thing, then look at the fancy cars, the neighbors or the roofs of houses!

- Listen to the birds, the traffic or the silence. Just stop and listen. How long has it been since you listened to the sounds of silence?

- Plan a vacation day. Take one day where you don't clean the house, work from home, or do errands. Take a day and go to a museum, or the beach or golf course.

- Go on a date. It could be a date with the girls, a date with your special someone, or hang out with the guys.

- Stop at the grocery store and buy dinner to go. A roasted chicken, salad, and a nice glass of wine is a perfectly healthy dinner and inexpensive when you buy them ready-to-go at a grocery store.

We need to stop out-busying each other. The next time someone asks you how you are, tell them you're "perfectly calm, in control and feeling pretty darned good, thank you." I can guarantee that they will not want to out-busy you then!

Are You Sleeping Enough?

I'm guessing that the most commonly asked question everyday is, "How Are You?" I'm also guessing that the most common answer is, "Fine." However, I'm willing to go out on a limb and say that the second most common response is "I'm a little tired."

How often have you said that? I personally have used that line, oh, just a few times. In our pursuit of a decent work/life ratio, here's something to consider: how much sleep is enough?

The experts tell us that we need between six to eight hours of sleep each night! That is not six to eight hours spent in bed, it is actually sleeping! How many of you are clock-watchers? I am. That means that several times each night, I roll over and look at the clock, just to see what time it is. It doesn't take me long to get back to sleep, but it does definitely interrupt my sleep patterns. On work nights, I can guess the time accurately (within about thirty minutes) *before* I look at the clock. Are any of you like that? It really makes me wonder how many hours of sleep I actually get. I think that it's funny that we can be so sleepy when we do this, yet our brain is wide-awake. Can't you immediately calculate (to the second) how much time we have left to sleep?

If you have ever read anything on sleep, you know that we have different stages of sleep. Well, if we keep waking up to look at the clock, we go through each stage several times each night. This interferes with the amount of quality sleep we get.

I have met several people who say they live on very little sleep. And, for a while, we all can. But not over the long term. Have you ever driven home and not remembered how you got there? (Scary isn't it?). Your body was physically working, but your brain was a million miles away (sleeping). We can train ourselves to live on less sleep, but over time, our bodies will rebel. Physical stress will result from a lack of sleep. You will suffer, your work will suffer, and your loved ones will definitely suffer!

So tonight, instead of watching the news at night—go to bed. Get yourself organized before you go to bed so you don't spend the night planning on what you have to do in the morning. Make lunches, set out clothes, get the car keys at the door ready to go, get the coffee pot ready, and make sure there is a towel at the shower! You will sleep better if you know everything is taken care of. Isn't funny how well we sleep on Friday night (when we don't have to get up Saturday morning)? When we are working all night long in our sleep, we are not getting six to eight hours of quality sleep.

You deserve to have your body and your brain healthy. All the stuff that keeps us up at night is either not important (mindless television) or it will wait (laundry, dishes, cleaning will all be there in the morning!). By taking care of yourself by getting enough sleep, you will have more energy to do these tasks later.

Sweet Dreams.

Do You Know How to Relax?

Closely related to sleep is the ability to relax. We get so wound up with work that we forget that we have to let go for awhile. Relaxation means various things to various people. Taking a walk in the country can be very relaxing; so can soaking in a hot bubble bath after a long day. When I use the word "relaxation," I am referring to a state of being, initiated by you, in which there are physiological and psychological changes. Just feeling relaxed may not mean that you are. It can be very frustrating not to be able to relax (and of course, very stressful and even unhealthy).

Think about what your perfect day "away from work" would consist of. Perhaps it is lazing around in bed until noon, maybe sitting in front of the television watching mindless television and even perhaps puttering in the garden pulling weeds. Whatever you would like to do on a day off is relaxing for you. Remember, this is not what you "should" do, it is what you "want" to do. They are different things!

We all relax differently, but we all definitely need to relax on a regular basis. In my Stress Management courses, I suggest that we each take thirty minutes every day to do something you truly enjoy doing (and find relaxing). Now this thirty minutes is consecutive (thirty one-minute increments do not count!). You must also be awake—and it isn't usually on company time (ha). Make sure you are getting this thirty minutes every day. My thirty minutes of relaxation time is spent right before I go to sleep—I read. I love to read, and make a point to do so every night; regardless of what time I go to bed.

Regularly practicing relaxation techniques can help you balance and heal the body and mind. Relaxation is a fundamental part of any stress management program. The beauty of mastering relaxation is that it allows you to voluntarily produce an alternative to the stress response and reverse its negative effects. It really does let you escape (even if it is just thirty minutes) from the stresses of our everyday environment.

Relaxation is good for you. It's a much-needed activity for over-stimulated bodies and minds. Under stress, your muscles tense, breathing becomes shallow, heart rate increases, blood pressure elevates, fat is released into the system. During relaxation, the opposite happens.

Have you relaxed today?

The Benefit to Relaxation: It Recharges Your Batteries

I've just shared with you how important relaxation is to being healthy. I'm really serious about this, so much so that I want you to make a resolution with me—even if it isn't New Years when you read this. And I really want you to intend to keep this one. It doesn't involve losing weight, exercising, or quitting smoking. At least not directly. I'm talking about resolving to regularly "recharge your batteries." Let's make some concrete and realistic plans that we can follow through with.

Be honest with yourself. How much "recharging" do you do in a week, a month, a year? Most of us have somehow got ourselves into situations where we are filling up every waking hour of every day doing "stuff," and much—too much—of that time is spent working. The time that isn't spent working is spent on maximizing every waking hour. At least for most of us, that is. And when we've finished filling up our personal and professional schedules, we sometimes feel the need to start working on our children's s chedules. We get busy filling up every spare moment that they have to keep them out of trouble, or to keep them from becoming bored. They are enrolled in hockey, soccer, swimming, piano... It seems as if we aren't "happy" until their days, and therefore ours, are completely full. In no way does this make us bad parents. But it does make us incredibly "busy" parents. Parents whose health, happiness, and sanity are often adversely affected by the hectic schedules that we impose on ourselves.

Back twenty years ago, predictions told us that we would probably be working a four-day work week by now. Are you working four days a week? Are you getting more time to spend with your family? The work week is actually getting longer, family time has decreased, and so stress levels have skyrocketed—all because we do not take the time to recharge our batteries.

I just told you earlier that you should spend thirty minutes every day relaxing. This actually takes that concept one step further. Schedule your "recharging" days or weeks into your yearly calendar. Do something you enjoy. Take time to "smell the roses." Spend time with family. Spend time with yourself. Read a book. Watch a sunset and a sunrise. Take the time to recharge your personal batteries so this can be a healthy year for you, both personally and professionally.

If you don't schedule the time, it will not magically appear. Take a couple of weekends for just your family. Schedule them into the calendar the same way we schedule meetings at work. Also, make sure to take a few days for you and you alone. For example, put time into your schedule for gardening. Perhaps you need to put the day in the schedule where you plant your tulips, or spend a day walking in the woods. Maybe you need to plan a day at the spa or shopping.

It's not as hard as you think, and the consequences of not doing so are very high, and not very pleasant. The way that we recharge our batteries is completely individual. Relaxing, as I said, is not the same for everyone. However, the need to recharge is mandatory.

If you don't make a commitment to recharge those batteries, they will run out of energy. Don't wait for that to happen, do something about it today.

So when you are planning your day, your week, your month, even your year, build some time on your schedule for you. It is important to relax each day so that we can tackle the world the next day! It's not selfish—it's preventative maintenance (which is common sense isn't it?).

The Pursuit of Balance

Relax, smell the roses, take a bath…sure Rhonda, you're saying, you can do all those things. I can't! I'm tearing my hair out trying to get everything done I need to.

Trust me. I know because I've been there. What I really am trying to get you to see here is that it's really all about balance. We must work. That is a fact of our society.

There was a movie a few years ago called *The Pursuit of Happyness*, starring Will Smith. He plays a man desperate to get a full-time job as a stockbroker. In order to maximize his working time, he goes to work early, he doesn't drink water (so he won't waste time going to the washroom), and he doesn't hang up the phone between calls (to save eight minutes a day). He does this so that he can be successful, so that he can provide for his son. I applaud him for his willingness to do anything he needed to make it happen for him—but at the end of the movie, I wondered if he was able to let go of some of his drive and remember that life is not all about work.

WORK/LIFE BALANCE

That's what it comes down to. It's why I've been guiding you down the path of relaxing, doing "nothing" for a little bit each day. Let me ask you a question: do you feel there is a fair distribution between your work and personal life? Notice I said "fair" balance, not "equal" balance.

Not everyone feels the same way about balance, relaxation, and the priority their job should have in their life.

My father is perfectly clear on what work/life balance means to him. He starts at 7:00 a.m. on the dot and finishes on time. He takes all of his lunches and breaks and he only works overtime if it is paid and pre-arranged. He cannot imagine why anyone would work as many hours as I do, or that anyone would allow their work life and personal life to intersect.

I can't imagine what a black-and-white approach to work/life would be like, and I'm pretty sure it wouldn't work for me. I love what I do, and I often have to pull myself away from my desk and stop working. When I've got nothing to do, no one to spend time with, or nothing that is grabbing my attention, I find myself gravitating towards my office. I like being on top of things, being proactive. That is the kind of balance that works for me.

So, let's look at what balance means for me. Have you ever had a sleepless night when all you did was worry about what you had to do at work? I have. That's why I check my e-mail at night before I go to bed. It actually helps me relax and not worry about the next day. Experts would say that I don't have balance, but for me, it works.

Immigration Canada called for a BlackBerry blackout recently. No more BlackBerry use from 7:00 p.m. to 7:00 a.m. or on weekends or holidays. They've even been banned from meetings. This is tough for me. I don't want to be told that I "have" to have my Black-Berry on when I'm living my personal life, but I also don't want to be told that I can't check it if I want to, either.

Balance. You have to find your own sense of what balance is for you. What I do know is it involves doing something that you enjoy. Not because you should, but because you enjoy it and want to.

Here's an example from my own life. I like to iron. (You may laugh at my enjoyment of ironing—no really, go ahead!) I'm also not a television junkie, but I do like reality television. I make sure that at least one evening a week, I turn something on television that I enjoy, pull out my ironing board and iron while watching TV for a couple of hours. I like this. It keeps my evenings in balance.

Here's another example: running on the treadmill is not something I enjoy. So when I go to the gym, I'll read a book, watch television or daydream. I need to exercise, but I can do something that I "have" to do and create balance at the same time.

THE ART OF REGAINING YOUR BALANCE

I also recognize that this quest for balance doesn't come easy. I run out of time every day. I sometimes wish there were thirty-four hours in a day because that extra ten hours would allow me to do some of the things I want to get done. When I don't get those things done I feel I have let people down.

We are also living in an era in which we want the fancy careers that come complete with the big paychecks, the nice cars, and the extravagant vacations. Yet we also want to have that picture-perfect family, a clean house, freshly pressed clothes each morning and the occasional dinner that is cooked rather than just reheated. Trust me, I often feel like I'm being pulled in a dozen different directions.

A couple of years ago, *The Wall Street Journal* surveyed more than eight hundred business professionals and found that those who focused on creating a balance between career and personal interests said they were most satisfied with their lives. People who said they were focused primarily on family or on work tended to be less satisfied. The question remains: How do we achieve a healthy balance?

Perhaps the easiest way to achieve balance is to constantly ask yourself: "does this action help me with balance or not?" And if not, "why am I doing it?"

Here are the larger questions behind work/life balance. They involve understanding what is most important to you and making time in your life for those things. The best way to proceed is to actually put your answers in writing. Ask yourself:

- What is important to you, and what would you like to have more of in your life? This should cover all areas of your life. Make sure you put in "time for me" if that is important. If you want an annual family vacation, or you want to cut the grass yourself each week, then those should be included. Perhaps you want to become a vice-president, and maybe you don't, but decide what is important to you.

- How can I make space for these things in my life? It's likely that in order to make space you will have to give something up. Are you willing to do that? I love to have time in my bathtub. I consider it a decadent experience, yet it is important to me that I spoil myself occasionally. But if I pour myself a bath at 8:00 p.m., I feel like I am taking time away from my family. And I am. But if I want my leisurely bath, I have to give something else up. The best route to take is to find the times that have the least impact on my family—for instance, after the kids are asleep or on the weekend. That way I get what I want and so do they. That's balance.

- What things are taking up too much space in your life? In the past, cleaning my house fell into this category. I felt that I could be doing other things that were more important to me, and cleaning was one of the things that took too much space. So I hired someone to do my cleaning. I had to give something up—money—but I got something in return, more quality time for myself.

Your attitude about balance also makes a big difference. Do you "have" to do things at home? Do you "have" to check your e-mail, your voice mail, your BlackBerry, or even work overtime? Or, do you "want" to do these tasks so that you can enjoy your non-work time even more? Stop worrying about what the experts say balance means. Spend more time thinking about what works best for you.

Understanding the things that are most important to you is the first step to achieving work/life balance. Making room for them, and perhaps giving up something to do that, is the second step. Then, continually confirming your priorities and actively making the attempt to keep balance in your life will help to keep you On-The-Right-Track!

PART FIVE

Success is Celebrating You

In the introduction, I told you that I wanted to help you be successful at work. I hope that you find my advice useful, and that it leads you to the success you want and deserve.

But before I leave you to your own common sense devices, I want to take a hard look now at what *success* is. Success, like many of the things I've talked about in here, is defined individually. Some define success by having lots of money, fancy cars, and big houses. Others know it to be a sense of accomplishment or even happiness.

Common practice, as we know, isn't something to trust anymore because it's gotten so far away from common sense. But common practice around the idea of success is really all over the board.

What I want you to look at in this section is how you define success. In doing so, I want you to take a hard look at where you are now, if you're happy in what you do, if you need to push yourself onward and upward or if you need to shake things up a bit.

But no matter where you are or what you need to do in your life, I want you to also make sure that you celebrate you—the successes you've had and that you will go on to achieve. I want you to give yourself a hearty pat on the back for who you are and what you do. As the commercial says, "you're worth it." So let's get on with it, shall we?

How Do You Define Success?

Whether you are successful or not depends largely on your definition of success. To use society's definition, success comes with a big paycheck, a fancy car, a prestigious address and an abundance of money. Is that success for you? Perhaps those would be some of the things you would have if you were successful, but is that how you define it? Probably not.

I was recently delivering a training session in which we were discussing success and ways in which our personal definitions were different from society's. Words like *self-satisfaction, balance, challenge, restful sleep, relaxation time,* and *contentment* were used. That concept of success is quite different from the "money, money, money" one.

Why is it that we judge how successful we are by the response of other people? Why do television and magazine articles tell us that we need to acquire "things" to be successful? Why do we all need to constantly earn more money to be considered successful? Why can't love be enough? I think it can be—we just need to adjust our views on success.

BEING A SUCCESS VERSUS BEING SUCCESSFUL

There is a sign that I have driven past (in Barrie, Ontario, I think) that says "Success is a journey…not a destination."

One of the things that I have noticed is the fact that our views of success will change many times in our lives. We have to be able to change with them or we will forever be unhappy. We have to stop trying to obtain success in the monetary ways that society measures success. We need to know what makes us happy, and consider that a success.

Let me give you some examples of success from my family. I know that for my son, he is successful when he beats his video game. Success to him is not necessarily getting all his math questions done right or done on time. Success is scoring a goal on his brother as they play street hockey. If you ask him if he had a successful day, it depends on how much fun he had and very little on how well he did that day.

My mom runs a golf snack bar. Her days are successful when she is able to keep the coffee fresh, the sandwiches made, and get the golfers in and out of the pro shop in less than two minutes. Her day isn't successful if it rains and there are thirty golfers waiting for a grilled cheese at the same time.

My day is successful when I get to almost see the bottom of the pile on my desk. If I walk out of my office and the pile is not bigger than when I walked in, it was a successful day. When I am delivering a keynote speech or a day of training, my day is considered successful if people felt that they learned something new, or they had a great time just participating and learning. It is not a successful day when someone falls asleep in my class. Is that fair? Maybe, maybe not. It could be that they were up all night long with a sick child and had to come to work the next day. It could be that the fact that they were sleeping had no reflection on how interesting my talk was. But to me, it was.

Now, to be totally honest when I define success for myself, I realize that some of the trappings of society enter into it. Does my car really matter? Well, I do drive a nice car, and I'm quite proud of it. Does owning it make me successful? Not really, but it does make me feel successful. Although consciously, I realize that money does not make someone successful, it can make one *feel* successful. If you feel successful, then you act successful. If you act successful you are treated by others as successful...and so on. So, part of my definition of success is what society considers successful as well. But I am clear that this is a small part of my own definition.

What it comes down to is that there seems to be two large categories of success: being a success and being successful. All the examples I just gave you are about being a success in a particular situation or in one day. Being successful is a big picture thing. For me, it's being at peace with myself. It's having time to do the little things that make the people around me feel valued, important and special, and doing them because I want to, not because I should. Balance is a big part of success for me, as you might imagine. I am a mother, wife, daughter, sister, aunt, and friend. I want to fit all of those roles into my life, as well as that of successful business owner.

DEFINING SUCCESS FOR YOU

Now it's your turn. I invite you to sit down with a pen and paper and decide what success is for you. Include material possessions, if they would be included in your definition of success. Don't apologize for it, either. Many of us are influenced by society far more than we want to admit, but that's okay because that may be part of you being a success. When you get down to defining what "being successful" means to you, think about the characteristics of success you want to have. What does a successful person look like to you? What do successful people do? How can you pick them out of a crowd? That can help you decide on your definition of success.

And then there's the following poem, often misattributed to American Essayist, Ralph Waldo Emerson, but was written by Bessie A Stanley:

To laugh often and much; to win the respect of intelligent people and affection of children; to earn the appreciation of honest critics and endure the betrayal of false friends; to appreciate beauty, to find the best in others; to leave the world a bit better, whether by a healthy child, or a garden patch or a redeemed social condition; to know even one life has breathed easier because you have lived. This is to have succeeded.[5]

So today, don't measure your success by what others think. Go back to being a kid when a successful day was one where you had fun. Avoid trying to compare yourself to others. Be sure to smile. Think about Ms. Stanley's definition and see if you're closer to her ideas of success than you originally thought.

When you have defined what success is for you, go to the mirror and look at yourself. Do you see a successful person staring back at you? I'm willing to bet that you will. Remember, in order to be seen by others as a success, you have to see it in yourself first.

---

[5] *Heart Throbs, Volume Two,*. ed. Joseph Mitchell Chapple. Boston: Chapple Publishing Company, 1911, pp. ii, 1-2. Surprisingly, "What is Success" is attributed to "Anon" in the index.

Are You Good Enough?

Do you ever sit back and look at life and say, "This is perfect?" I hope that occasionally this happens to you, that you are perfectly satisfied, that life is exactly what you pictured it to be, and that you are truly happy.

When we're talking success, though, what we cannot ever do is settle for "good enough." "Good enough" is the enemy of great. People just accept that this will do. Now don't get me wrong, I believe we should be happy with what we have. We just can't become complacent about it. Don't ever get to the point where you stop growing as an individual. Don't ever say "but that's the way it has always been."

Years ago, I became complacent with my job. At the time I had a toddler at home; I was making good enough (not great, but good enough) money, and I knew my job really well. I was able to be up all night long with Christopher if necessary, and still perform well in my job. I was good enough. The problem was that I stopped grow-ing as an employee and as a person.

Well, when this company downsized (something many of us have experienced) I quickly realized that "good enough" for ABC Company wasn't good enough for anyone else. I really looked at my qualifications and realized what I had done. Three years earlier, I was very qualified to move around if necessary. When I started to become complacent, my skills very quickly became average, normal, every-day stuff! In a tough economy that makes finding another job (especially the well paid ones) very difficult to do.

My son Patrick is one of those students who can get a straight "B" average without ever studying or doing homework. Once when his report card came, it was straight "B's" because he had put zero effort into his homework. When we asked him what he thought about it, his response was "It's good enough." His father and I didn't need to say much. Patrick realized that that wasn't good enough for mom and dad. He could have come home with all C's and I would have been thrilled if he had put effort into it. The actual mark wasn't important; it was the "good enough" attitude that we didn't like.

Is your life where you want it to be, or is it "good enough"? Do yourself a favor and put a little effort into making your own decisions and choices. You'll be pleasantly surprised and motivated to be true to yourself.

Are You Ignoring Your Own Thirst?

I just told you that you need to make your own decisions and choices to avoid the "good enough" syndrome. But that's not always the easiest thing to do—there are consequences attached to any decision we make, especially at work. Consider this, though— *The Harvard Business Review* reported, "Making decisions is one of our most important jobs. It is also the toughest and the riskiest. Bad decisions can damage a business and a career, sometimes irreparably."[6] Bad decisions affect our ability to keep our job or to even stay in business. They can significantly affect our careers.

As business professionals, one way that we can up the ante on keeping ourselves fresh and out of the "good enough" syndrome is to always be maximizing our skills to ensure we are making the right decisions. But that begs the question (and I know you were thinking it…). How are you ensuring that you are always making good decisions?

Well, let me ask some questions in response to yours: Are you involved in any formal or informal networking groups? Do you belong to any associations? Does your company provide continuing education? Do you attend company training events (or do you tell yourself you don't have time)? Do you just trust what you've learned in the past and your "gut reaction" to help you make good decisions?

It continues to amaze me how many people re-invent the wheel every day. In this process they often make some very bad

---

6   *Harvard Business Review on Making Smarter Decisions* (Paperback). Boston: HBR, 2007.

decisions. With a small up-front investment in time, they could save themselves a lot of decision time by learning from the experiences of others.

Many companies follow the same "limited-thinking" thought process and do not provide sufficient training, networking or educational opportunities for their employees. Shame, shame I say! Regardless, if your company doesn't pay for these opportunities, seek them out yourself. It is worth your own time and dollar investment to keep your business skills current and useful. What will happen if your company doesn't need you any more? You will look back at your "excuses" about why you didn't do anything and realize this was a very bad decision.

On the other hand, those who are proactive go looking for information may become overloaded with advice—everything from "go vegetarian," to "high-meat protein diets are best," or "do work at home to get the important things done," to "never allow yourself to take work home." We are consistently being given a multitude of choice. We hear conflicting advice as well as corroborating advice. What do we typically do with this advice? Listen and then ignore it.

In order for us to be successful we need to take risks and make decisions based on this advice. Are you guilty of attending continuing education programs, workshops or seminars after which your notes get piled in a corner and are never looked at again?

Why do we do that? Sometimes it feels as if we are drinking from a fire hydrant. We need water, but we drown ourselves in this water. The next time we are thirsty, we are hesitant to go back to the fire hydrant. Are you pulling away from getting additional information because it has felt like drinking from a fire hydrant?

Are you being given so much information about the decisions you need to make that you are paralyzed with information?

Instead of avoiding the fire hydrant, why don't we decide to drink just what we need instead of trying to drink it all?

I encourage you to decide what skills and information you need. It could be as simple as basic time management or conflict management skills training or as complex and time-consuming as needing to attain a university degree. If you know what you are looking for, it is easy to find. When you don't know what you are looking for, it is like taking a drink from a fire hydrant. I want you to succeed, not drown! Once you decide to take action and start searching for new information, you will find it (I promise).

Stuck in a Rut?
Here's How to Get Off the Nail

One of the biggest problems in our quest for success is that we get into a job with good pay, good benefits, that sort of thing, and then….we get stuck. Research tells us that two out of every three people are dissatisfied with their job.

Why do people stay in a job they don't like? Probably because it easier to stay than it is to go and look for another job. They're stuck in a rut.

I once heard a story about a woman who walked by a certain house every day. There was a man on the porch, and a dog lying at his feet. Every day the woman heard the dog moaning and groaning, clearly uncomfortable. One day, the woman asked the man, "Why is your dog always moaning?" The man said, "He's lying on a nail."

That dog was uncomfortable, but just not quite uncomfortable enough to actually get up and move. That's what it's like to be stuck in a rut. You're not really happy, but you're not quite unhappy enough to make a change.

Part of the "good enough" syndrome—the one that keeps us from being truly successful—is we're afraid of the unknown. We will more often than not choose the devil we know over the devil we don't know.

IT'S A PROFESSIONAL MID-LIFE CRISIS

I had a professional mid-life crisis at the tender age of twenty-eight. I started out loving my job—I was getting paid well and was successful at my job. Then, without realizing it, I drifted into the comfort zone. I could work for a whole morning on automatic pilot. Life was easy, and comfortable—too comfortable. The problem arose when I stayed in that comfort zone too long. My life went from comfortable to stuck—in a professional rut. I was in a professional mid-life crisis. My job was easy, I liked my colleagues, the money was great, and I had no reason to change anything, except that my job no longer satisfied me.

How do you get over a professional mid-life crisis? Through focus, goal-setting, positive thinking and career counseling. For me, the focus and goal-setting were the most important elements. I asked myself, "What would I do as a job if money wasn't an issue?"

Ask yourself these questions:

- Do I dislike going to work?
- Do I think I should probably look for another job, but am afraid to?
- Am I envious of people who enjoy what they do?
- Do I feel that underutilized in my current position?
- Am I afraid that my skills will no longer be relevant in the marketplace?

I recently spent some time with "Mary" who is in precisely this situation. She has worked at the same company for fifteen years. She generally enjoys her job but has become a little bored recently. To make matters worse, there has been significant turnover at her firm and her team isn't the same anymore. She is wondering whether it is time for her to leave. Actually, she's been asking herself that question for the past several years, but she justifies staying: her job is comfortable, the commute is manageable, the money is competitive, her paid holiday-time is starting to add up, the company needs her and, with fifteen years of job security, she is afraid to start at the bottom of the tenure ladder again.

Is she stuck? Yes, and she really does know it, but fear keeps her from acting on it.

Are you a motivated person who has reached the top at your company? Are you going to work for the people rather than the job? Are you "too" loyal? Have you stayed in the same position (title or salary range) for more than five years?

Maybe you are also stuck.

Don't get me wrong, if you love what you do, and realize that what we're saying here doesn't pertain to you, don't worry if you've been in the same job forever. You aren't stuck if you love it, and it isn't bad to stay in the same job for a long time either.

But if you truly are stuck in a rut, here is what you need to do:

EXAMINE YOUR MOTIVES

Are you doing what you're doing because of the money, or because it works well with your family schedule, or the commute is easy? If you love what you do enough, those other components won't matter.

Why did you take your job in the first place? If the answer is money, you may be in trouble. The same way you shouldn't marry some-one for money, you shouldn't take a job just because it pays well. There has to be more to the job than just the paycheque.

Think back to when you started your job. What part of it did you love the most? What part did you get excited about? You can find ways to get those elements back into your daily work life.

Ask yourself what you would be doing if money wasn't an issue. Would it be your current job? If not, it may be time to face up to your mid-life professional crisis that has put you into a rut. Here's how:

- **Focus.** Spend some time thinking about your current job and your reasons for taking the job in the first place. Think about your job's pros and cons.

- **Re-examine your goals.** Are they still relevant? If not, it's time to come up with some new ones.

- **Stay positive.** Change may be painful in the short-term, but if it gets you out of a rut, it's a good thing in the long run. Think of this as a positive time; you're doing something good for yourself.

- **Seek advice.** If you're still in a rut, seek advice from a career counselor or trusted mentor or friend.

Imagine going in to work each day, loving the job you do and enjoying every minute of it. Here are some pointers on how to find a "dream" job, even if you're not looking:

- **Surf the job posting sites.** Check out monster.ca (or monster.com), Workopolis or other sites pertinent to your area of expertise to see if you find anything that totally excites you. Apply for five jobs that are completely out of your range. If they ask for a university degree and you don't have one, apply anyway. If they ask for you to have ten years of experience, and you don't, apply anyway. If they ask you to be bilingual, and you aren't really, apply anyway.

- **Scare yourself.** What have you got to lose by applying for jobs you won't get? You might not get an interview. That's fine, because this is about scaring yourself more than it is about getting a new job. If you get the interview, go! Practice your skills. Learn how to be interviewed so that when the perfect opportunity presents itself you will be prepared.

· **Start looking for that "perfect" job.** Once you are comfortable with the above process (and it may take a few months), start looking in newspapers. If you find the perfect job (or something pretty close), apply for it. Make a serious effort to get the interview.

· **Start networking.** After you are comfortable with really looking for a new job, start contacting headhunters, placement companies, and let people know that you are open to new opportunities. Networking is absolutely the best way to get a new opportunity.

None of this means you have to say "yes" to any job offers. What it allows you to do is to make choices calmly, slowly, and logically.

When the right door opens for you, you will know that you are supposed to walk through it. If it doesn't feel like it is the best choice for you, don't make it. Wait until you are sure.

The most important point here is if you face up to your professional mid-life crisis in a positive and courageous way, your life can be the same!

You won't get unstuck immediately. It will take some tire spinning, as well as a desire for a new adventure. It will take risk and faith to get unstuck. But you will find that leaving your comfortable situation will be one of the best choices you ever make.

So go on—get off the nail. Life is far too long for you to settle for anything less than what makes you really happy.

Get Your Mojo Back

I'm getting married! We bought a house! We're having a baby! I got accepted into university! Remember those moments? Remember how excited, how full of energy, how positive you were?

When you start feeling the "good enough" syndrome coming on, it also does something else besides keeping you stuck on that painful rut of a nail. You may not realize it, but it's zapping that fabulous energy, the kind that made you wanted to jump out of bed in the morning because you were so excited about what was on your schedule.

If you are like most people, those events occurred sometime in your twenties or early thirties. There are many years between those events and the words, "I'm retiring!" Most of the days in those intervening years are the "good enough" years. We get caught up in the day-to-day chores of going to work, raising a family, watching TV, and sleeping. We seem to put our lives on hold for twenty or thirty years, waiting for the next big event—retirement—to come along.

The danger of this holding pattern is boredom. Boredom sinks in and everyone and everything looks better than what we have. Even so, we don't bother to shake things up in order to get more. We achieve all of our goals. We've done "it"—whatever "it" is—now what?

We need to regenerate the positive energy we feel when there's a big event coming up, and let that excitement spill over into all areas of our lives. For some, as I said above, it might be going out and finding that "perfect" job. But, say you really like your job and are feeling stuck anyway. What can you do? Plenty! You need to get motivated in your professional and personal lives. Here are some suggestions:

CREATING THAT "BIG EVENT"

Take up a new hobby or sport. Plan to get good at it. Don't decide that this is the year you are going to learn to play golf, plan on this being the year you break 100 in golf (or ninety!). Set a goal that causes you to really work hard at it.

Start planning next year's vacation now. Don't wait until the last minute. Research every possible destination, every option, every up-grade. Take the time to enjoy planning the trip. Get excited about it.

Take a course or two at your local college or university. Something you are interested in, something that will stretch your brain and get you excited. Perhaps you will never actually get your law degree, but who says you can't take a couple of courses in criminal law? Plan your graduation—in 2020—and be excited about it!

Maybe it's your relationship that's in a holding pattern. Plan a second honeymoon. Do something for the two of you that you used to do when you were dating. Do something you haven't done in a long time. Take the time to plan it. Get excited, motivated, and energized about your relationship. Lots of marriages fall apart due boredom. Don't be a statistic.

Sometimes, even just dusting off your resume will help you understand why you are stuck. It doesn't mean you have to go out and get a new job, but maybe it will help you understand why you are stuck. When you look your career on paper, it is often very obvious, and you'll know what to do. Ask yourself this simple question: "If you could do anything in the world, what would it be?" Then, find a way to do it, even if it is in your spare time. Stop digging your rut deeper. Find the time to motivate yourself, and stop justifying your boredom.

What I want for you is to find that excitement in the years between youth and retirement. The journey of finding what that is will keep us motivated. But whatever "it" is, I want you to find a constant source of mojo, the stuff that keeps us young, energized, and alive.

You are Either Living or You are Dying. Which are You Doing?

In the movie *The Shawshank Redemption*, the main character says that there is one choice to make in life: We can either get busy living or get busy dying. If you aren't actively doing one of these then you are, by default, doing the other. If you aren't excited about life, then, by this dictum, you're headed south. I meet so many people who are passively dying. They're in a "comfort zone," a bit different than a rut because those in the comfort zone are on autopilot, just getting by.

Have you ever driven somewhere and not remembered how you got there? You put yourself on automatic pilot, turning off your brain for the mundane task of driving. Many people do that at work. They sit back and relax into their comfort zone, allowing their body to perform mundane tasks automatically and giving their mind the day off. They ask nothing of their brain, and as a result it becomes more and more comfortable doing very little active thinking at all. Before they know it, these people start to die inside. Are you allowing yourself to die at work? I hope not. But, if you are, here are some suggestions on what you can do about it:

GETTING YOUR DREAM JOB

Imagine you just won $100,000, enough money to allow you to quit your current job for a while, but you'd eventually have to get another one. In other words, the perfect opportunity to get out of your comfort zone and make some changes. What would you do? What is your dream job? Does your current job offer any of those opportunities? If not, can you go looking for them? Most jobs offer many opportunities, although we tend to tell ourselves we don't have the time to take advantage of them. But if your will to live is strong enough, you will make the time.

Working is a fact of life for most people. But so is eating vegetables to stay healthy. I personally don't like to eat peas very often. It would make no sense for me to cook them every night would it? So, if I have to eat vegetables, I look around for a vegetable that I do like, and I cook it. If I have to work, I should look around for parts of my job that I do like and focus on those instead of forcing myself through the actions just because I have to work.

HOW TO GET OUT OF THE COMFORT ZONE

List the ten duties or activities of your job you like best (don't list: break, lunch, or time to go home). Find ways to do those activities more often, perhaps join a committee or team that will require those activities. It will be more work and effort than before, but living takes more effort. On the plus side, if you are living at work, the days will go by much faster than when you were slowing dying.

FOCUS ON WHAT YOU LOVE ABOUT YOUR JOB

Don't dwell on what you don't like about your job. Trade some of your duties at work. If you don't like making client follow-up calls and your co-worker doesn't like attending meetings, see if it is realistic to trade. Draft your "dream job." What does it look like? Take one activity at a time and try to incorporate it into your job.

HOW I STARTED LIVING IN MY JOB

Here is an example of what I have done in the past: When I was younger, I always wanted to travel. I thought it sounded like a lot of fun and was something I'd always had on my to-do list. The job I was in at the time involved no travel at all. Another job in my company became available in a different department. Still no travel involved. However, there were people in that department who did travel. I made a lateral transfer to that department. I learned about the department, about the travel and about the other jobs in the department. The next time one of the positions that required travel was available, I applied for it and I got it.

I made a strategic decision to work towards something positive in my job. It took time and effort, but I stayed focused on what I wanted and I started living! My desire to be alive professionally was so strong that I made the time to ensure I got what I wanted. If I had never made those efforts and had continued to sit in my other job saying things like, "I sure wish I had a job where I could travel," but had never done anything about it, I would have been dying inside.

Desire, plus the willingness to do something about it, equals living. No desire, or no desire to do anything about it, equals dying. Don't be one of the living dead.

Shake things up—and get living!

You're Never Too Old

There's a wonderful upside to choose living over dying. It means that you never have to say you're too old to try new things. Have you ever said that? To me, that idea almost physically hurts, because I like to think that I'm not too old for anything. Surprisingly enough, I do meet people who think they are "too old" to do things.

I recently switched to a Macintosh laptop. I have been using PC since the PC came into the work environment in the 1980s. I started out as a computer trainer, so I am extremely comfortable with the PC environment, and computers in general. My entire networked office is PC-based but I wanted a MacBookAir (for ease of travel—plus I love the commercial). I wasn't afraid to switch, but I was worried about the productivity time I would lose as I learned the "new" way of doing things.

I was explaining the rationale for my switch to a participant in one of my seminars and her comment was, "I'm too old to learn a new way of using a computer." I was actually speechless, because I think she is younger than I am. Of all the reasons to not switch, my age never came into the equation.

I remember when my mom was required to learn about computers for her job. She was very comfortable with the manual method and was afraid of learning how to use a computer. She justified it by saying she was too old.

I know that many people feel trapped in their jobs because they feel they are too old to be hired by someone else, or to learn new skills.

I was telling someone about IAAP recently (International Association of Administrative Professionals www.iaap-hq.org) and encouraging her to join, for a multitude of reasons. Her response was that she was "too old for that sort of thing."

Are these excuses based in fear, or is there really such a thing as too old? Consider these "chronies":

- Clint Eastwood was seventy-four when he won the Best Director Oscar in 2004.

- Jack Weil worked daily at Rockmount Ranch Wear, where he was the CEO, until he was 107 years old.

- There is a sixty-five-year-old Indian woman who has given birth.

- Ernest Easton has always had an insatiable thirst for knowledge, and at eighty-nine he holds the honor of being the oldest person in the world to earn a Ph.D.

- In 1991 Minnie Munro became the world's oldest bride, at 102. Her groom was a sprightly eighty-three.

CLEARLY "TOO OLD" DOESN'T EXIST FOR SOME

Last week, when I went through airport security, the security man was scanning my carry-on luggage and remarked that my laptop was very sexy. For a split-second I thought he was complimenting me, and I certainly wasn't too old to hear that! Too old is just an excuse. What is there to be afraid of? Is it better to have tried and failed or to have never tried at all? I am, naturally, on the side of trying and failing. I urge you to put your fears aside and never be on the side of "afraid to try."

Do You Celebrate You?

When you look in the mirror in the morning, what do you see? Do you see the kind, caring person you are on the inside, or do you see that your nose is too big, you have a new grey hair or that there are wrinkles around your eyes?

What I'm talking about is, the last principle of success, no matter what you do or where you are in life. It's making sure to celebrate you!

"Celebrating you" does not necessarily make you the centre of the universe. It does not have to be selfish, egotistical or conceited. It does, however, make you a priority in your own life.

When was the last time you made yourself a priority or gave yourself a pat on the back? For most of us, it has been far too long. Celebrating you is important because if you can't celebrate your own worth, how will anyone else? You must see (and celebrate) it first.

Let's look at the end of this book as a new beginning, a New Years, of sorts. New Years usually come with resolutions complete with plans to change the person you are. Instead, in this beginning, I invite you to celebrate the person you are. As you plan the next twelve months, make yourself a priority. Celebrate what you do well and congratulate yourself on a job well done. Stop being your own worst enemy, telling yourself that you aren't good enough, you can't do it, or that someone is better than you.

Celebrating your physical self can be one place to start. Another is the professional you. Do you celebrate you at work? Often when we make a mistake, rather than laughing it off or moving forward, we chide ourselves, "Sometimes you're such an idiot!" Intellectually we understand that we don't have to be perfect, and yet we are the first to criticize ourselves when we are less than perfect. That's quite a mixed message we send to ourselves. So while I spent some time talking about your work/life balance, this is ultimately a book about work, and it is very important to celebrate what you've accomplished in your work life.

A few years ago, I made the mistake of forgetting to celebrate me. Rather than simply asking to have my needs met, I hoped that the universe would know what I wanted and just give it to me. I was out of town when my birthday rolled around. Earlier, I had down-played my birthday to my friends by saying, "Don't worry about my birthday, it's no big deal. Don't make me a cake or anything." So they didn't. I was wished Happy Birthday, but otherwise nothing was done. I was actually very disappointed. I really thought that my friends knew me better than that. I didn't ask to have my own needs met, and I was the only one who suffered.

The real problem was, at that time, I wasn't celebrating me—and so no one else was, either. I learned a lot that year. I now know that I am worthy of my own attention and that if I want something I need to ask for it. And if I'm not given what I want, I am capable of finding another way to get it.

Celebrating you is simply looking inside and deciding that "I am worthy." It's summoning up our inner resources, rewarding what we do well, forgiving what we don't do well, and being the best "us" we can be. That's success, and that's something to celebrate.

It's easy to read through all my points and funny stories and say to yourself, "Oh, I knew that!" Of course you did, but what are you doing about it? It is a very uncomfortable task to look into the mirror and ask yourself if you are really following through with the common sense that you already know. Sadly, most people are following common practice and not common sense.

I'm sure we've all heard the expression "Do as I say, but not as I do." I'm sure we can all agree that isn't an expression we want to model our life after. We want to do the right thing, say the right thing and think the right thing. We want our thoughts, words and actions to be aligned. We want to be On-The-Right-Track all day and every day.

The good news is that we can! It does take some strategy. It takes a lot of patience and it takes commitment. The results will be worth every bit of effort that you put into them.

As I get older I look back on my life and wish I had done a few things a little differently. I still have many years ahead of me, and while I realize that although I will continue to make mistakes, I would rather make new mistakes than continue to replicate the old ones.

My mother taught me common sense. I pass it onto my children, and I now pass it onto you. Common sense tells me to apply the lessons I have already learned, and it tells me that you can too apply them too. It is up to you!

Good luck, and keep yourself ON THE RIGHT TRACK to professional and personal success!

About the Author

Rhonda Scharf, CSP

Insightful, humorous, entertaining, even contagious. These are the words that are often used to describe Rhonda Scharf, a speaker with the uncanny ability to look at the normal and see something quite different.

Rhonda is a Professional Speaker, Trainer, and Author. She has spoken to tens of thousands of people in seven different countries. Rhonda has served as the National President in 2004 for the Canadian Association of Professional Speakers (CAPS), has served on the Board of the International Federation of Professional Speakers, and is named in the current edition of "Who's Who in Professional Speakers," (where she has been listed since 1998).

Rhonda has been earning money from speaking since she was two years old! Her mother used to offer her twenty-five cents just to be quiet for five minutes. Since that time she has figured out how to get clients to pay her to speak and to not be quiet. Her mother and her family still don't understand why.

Rhonda has earned the highest speaking designation in the world, the "Certified Speaking Professional" designation (CSP). She was Canada's third female to earn this designation.

She is an avid social marketer, so be sure to link with Rhonda on FaceBook, LinkedIn, Plaxo and Twitter (all Rhonda Scharf). You will learn more about Rhonda both personally and professionally.

In her home just outside Ottawa, Ontario (Canada), she runs a busy household with four teenagers and one husband but unfortunately no time for animals! In her spare time, Rhonda likes to relax by camping, golfing, reading, vacationing, and... ironing!

Rhonda Scharf, CSP
Certified Speaking
Professional, Trainer, and
Author
www.on-the-right-track.com
1-877-213-8608

LaVergne, TN USA
28 August 2009
156213LV00004B/6/P